During the past forty years there has been an explosion of writings, both scientific and nonscientific, about the question of "identity" and what it means to be an individual in today's world. This book examines sociological perspectives on identity in order to illuminate the perennial problem of defining the human person, and to propose a new definition of identity based on its being socially constructed.

Beginning with a review of previous studies of identity, the authors present a set of propositions for organizing the wide range of uses of the term, and for arriving at an adequate definition of it. They then analyze identity in two contexts: one – gender identity – linked to present bodies, and the other – prenatal and postmortem identities – linked to future and past bodies. They show that whereas gender identity reveals the powerful but breakable link between body type and identity, prenatal and postmortem identities illustrate the symbolic reality and partial independence of identity from any corporeal existence. This analysis demonstrates the interpretive power of a theory of identity that views it as a reality constructed by human beliefs, actions, and artifacts in the process of people living together. It leads into a final chapter that raises a series of value issues about identity: Are some identities sacred and unquestionable? Are identities what make us real persons? Or are they mere masks that render us inauthentic?

The issues of identity and a meaningful life are crucial in the modern world. This innovative and insightful study will appeal to sociologists, social psychologists, and social philosophers concerned with understanding the nature of human identity and contribute to a sociological approach to generic issues in social psychology.

The Arnold and Caroline Rose Monograph Series
of the American Sociological Association

Society and identity

Other books in the series

J. Milton Yinger, Kiyoshi Ikeda, Frank Laycock, and Stephen J. Cutler: *Middle Start: An Experiment in the Educational Enrichment of Young Adolescents*

James A. Geschwender: *Class, Race, and Worker Insurgency: The League of Revolutionary Black Workers*

Paul Ritterband: *Education, Employment, and Migration: Israel in Comparative Perspective*

John Low-Beer: *Protest and Participation: The New Working Class in Italy*

Orrin E. Klapp: *Opening and Closing: Strategies of Information Adaptation in Society*

Rita James Simon: *Continuity and Change: A Study of Two Ethnic Communities in Israel*

Marshall B. Clinard: *Cities with Little Crime: The Case of Switzerland*

Steven T. Bossert: *Tasks and Social Relationships in Classrooms: A Study of Instructional Organization and Its Consequences*

Richard E. Johnson: *Juvenile Delinquency and Its Origins: An Integrated Theoretical Approach*

David R. Heise: *Understanding Events: Affect and the Construction of Social Action*

Ida Harper Simpson: *From Student to Nurse: A Longitudinal Study of Socialization*

Stephen P. Turner: *Sociological Explanation as Translation*

Janet W. Salaff: *Working Daughters of Hong Kong: Filial Piety or Power in the Family?*

Joseph Chamie: *Religion and Fertility: Arab Christian–Muslim Differentials*

William Friedland, Amy Barton, and Robert Thomas: *Manufacturing Green Gold: Capital, Labor, and Technology in the Lettuce Industry*

Richard N. Adams: *Paradoxical Harvest: Energy and Explanation in British History, 1870–1914*

Mary F. Rogers: *Sociology, Ethnomethodology, and Experience: A Phenomenological Critique*

James R. Beniger: *Trafficking in Drug Users: Professional Exchange Networks in the Control of Deviance*

Jon Miller: *Pathways in the Workplace: The Effects of Gender and Race on Access to Organizational Resources*

Society and identity

Toward a sociological psychology

Andrew J. Weigert
University of Notre Dame

J. Smith Teitge
Dennis W. Teitge

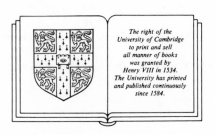

The right of the
University of Cambridge
to print and sell
all manner of books
was granted by
Henry VIII in 1534.
The University has printed
and published continuously
since 1584.

Cambridge University Press

Cambridge
London   New York   New Rochelle
Melbourne   Sydney

Published by the Press Syndicate of the University of Cambridge
The Pitt Building, Trumpington Street, Cambridge CB2 1RP
32 East 57th Street, New York, NY 10022, USA
10 Stamford Road, Oakleigh, Melbourne 3166, Australia

First published 1986

Printed in the United States of America

Library of Congress Cataloging-in-Publication Data
Weigert, Andrew J.
Society and identity.
(The Arnold and Caroline Rose monograph series of
the American Sociological Association)
Bibliography: p.
Includes index.
1. Identity.   2. Social role.   3. Sex role.
4. Symbolic interactionism.   I. Teitge, J. Smith (Joyce
Smith), 1949–   .   II. Teitge, Dennis W. (Dennis
Wayne), 1948–   .   III. Title.   IV. Series.
HM291.W45   1986   305.3   85-19026

British Library Cataloguing-in-Publication Data
Weigert, Andrew J.
Society and identity : toward a sociological
psychology. – (The Arnold and Caroline Rose
monograph series of the American Sociological
Association)
1. Identity   2. Social interaction
I. Title   II. Teitge, J. Smith   III. Teitge,
Dennis W.   IV. Series
302   HM291
ISBN 0 521 32325 8

To
Marie
Fred and Dorothy
Kathleen, Karen, and Sheila
Josh and Deni

Contents

Preface

Humans have always attempted to define themselves individually and collectively. Merely listing some essentially human characteristics evokes primeval memories of what we once thought of our selves. From ancient times, the individual has been ultimately defined by inexplicable or observable functions, remnants and fantasies of the bodily self. The human may be a "shade" inhabiting a body, a divine spark giving life to the body, a breath whose presence assured that life was present, or a psyche or mind that accounted for the individual's experience of mental reality. During the Christian era, many of these essences, purified of organic vestiges, came to be located in the idea of a soul, that totally spiritual entity that gave each person his or her individuality and transcendent existence.

After the Cartesian critique and the Enlightenment reformulation, the human person came to be thought of as a thinker of reason or a machine of matter. At the turn of the nineteenth century, American social thinkers, influenced by German romantic philosophers, adopted the language of the self to refer to the uniquely human component of such members of the animal kingdom. After the Darwinian impact, self was seen as emerging by the same natural laws operating in the rest of the biological world; and yet, with language and culture, humans acquire a different kind of consciousness – namely, self-consciousness. The social self is a concept that has been variously acceptable and unacceptable to both idealist and materialist interpreters of the human person. At about the same time, psychological thinkers were developing concepts such as ego, personality, and character to explain the psychic reality of the human person. Into these streams of thought, and quickly throughout contemporary American social and psychological commentary, came the recent concept of identity. In a real sense, we take the concept of identity as a descendant of the earlier attempts to answer the perennial questions: How do we define the human individual? Who are we?

As sociologists, we come to this issue with a general set of intellectual concerns. Like the meaning of any other object in our sociocultural context, the human individual is defined within the symbols and meanings available in our historical time. Furthermore, we take these meanings to be, at least in large part, socially constructed. In other words, intentional, interactional, structural, and cultural processes and objects enter into our definition of our selves and into the public definition of us by others. As we may put it aphoristically: Social organization is the principle of self-organization.

Our work in this area has a dual purpose. The direct and overriding goal is to shed light on the perennial issue of human definition. Indeed, we are convinced of the urgent relevance of Erik Erikson's informed insistence that the integrity and continuity of human identity is a defining feature of our times. Our indirect and secondary goal is to help develop a sociologically grounded approach to the generic issues of social psychology. We feel that such an approach is both vitally needed and sorely underdeveloped to date.

This book hazards a step or two toward our goals. First, we endeavor to present a preliminary historical understanding of the emergence and uses of identity within sociological social psychology. This is the task of Chapter 1. To be usable for a sociological enterprise, the concept of identity needs both theoretical articulation and empirical application. Chapter 2 attempts an initial codification and a nominal definition that brings together the main lines of writing about identity. The next two chapters move closer to the empirical moment. Chapter 3 builds on innovative and provocative work in the area of gender identity while formulating testable propositions relating homosexual identity and occupation. Chapter 4 takes us a step further toward a sociological understanding of identity by considering cases of identities without typical bodily presence, as in the cases of prenatal and postmortem identities. These considerations convince us of the relevance and power of a social constructionist approach to the issue of defining the human individual. We are eager to see if others feel the same. Finally, we end on the note that motivated us throughout: The issue of identity is a definitive feature of contemporary life.

We would like to thank Professor Suzanne Keller for seeing strengths in our original manuscript and for patience throughout the revision process. Thanks are also due to the anonymous reviewers for helping us to spill off some bathwater without losing the baby. The typing credits go to Ms. Shirley Schneck and the University of Notre Dame Faculty steno pool, especially Karen Kretschmer, Debra K. Nicodemus, and Sandy Superczynski.

Our thanks go also to JAI Press, Inc., for permission to use a slightly revised version of "Identity: its emergence within sociological psychology," *Symbolic Interaction* 6(2):183–206 (1983).

Finally, we would like to thank our parents, both of German and Native-American origin, who gave us a sense of our identities past, and our current families who are giving us our meaning of self and identity today.

PART I

The story of whence identity and a step toward theory

"Identity" is both a cultural cliché and a technical term in the interpretive vocabularies of social and psychological analysts in the early 1980s. A mere forty years before, the term was hard to find. The story of the emergence of identity in the work of sociological social psychologists is briefly told in Chapter 1. In spite of the schematic nature of the chapter, we believe the main outlines are clear. Powerful and different sources came together in a unique configuration. The social and psychological turmoil of World War II provided a historical context in which what we may call the identity question was asked in three different situations.

First, a nation of immigrants asked what it meant to be an American, both during a war against the mother countries of many of its citizens and in the following period of prosperity amid anxiety, punctuated by emancipatory social movements. Second, an intellectually and geographically migrating scholar moved across the national boundaries of German- and English-speaking worlds and across the intellectual boundaries of psychoanalytic and social anthropological paradigms; as he struggled to make sense out of his biography and to understand the character malaise of contemporary persons, Erik Erikson began formulating the concept of ego identity and articulating the problem of identity as characteristic of the modern world. Finally, a small group of sociologists working within a version of American pragmatism were trying to develop a more adequate sociological psychology for understanding human action as essentially social; they knew of Erikson's work and quickly adopted his term, but shortened it to "identity." Fueled by these three sources, identity was "in the air" by the 1960s and on everyone's tongue by the 1970s. As far as our preliminary investigation can uncover, the term indeed is propelled from Erikson's written formulations and collegial networks. Over the next twenty years, however, the term was used by sociologists working in five different theoretical traditions: processual and structural symbolic interactionism, sociology of knowledge, structural-functionalism,

1

and critical theory. Analysts investigating a host of social and psychological issues came to use identity as a conceptual tool.

Chapter 1 is not a technical history of an idea not the history of the emergence of a paradigm. As we see it, the paradigm already existed in critical social science – namely, that sociocultural factors shape the structure and content of human self-definition. The chapter does try to tell the story of the origin and diffusion of identity as *the* term for conceptualizing a distinctly sociological perspective on the perennial question of human self-definition. Furthermore, identity brings an enhanced sensitivity to structures and processes from the micro, cognitive, and interactional levels of analysis to the macro, ideological, and structural levels. Identity, then, serves as a contemporary formulation of a perennial human issue and a fruitful bridging concept for organizing work in sociological psychology.

Chapter 2 presents a series of general propositions and a definition of identity that outline a generic theory of identity. The orienting paradigm is that social reality is a human social production. This statement must be taken together with its triplet-born propositions: Social reality is a human production; social reality is an emergent reality, sui generis; and humans themselves are societal productions (see Berger and Luckmann 1966). This social constructionist paradigm tries to bring together the concepts of micro and macro, as well as processual and structural traditions in sociology. Identity cuts across these boundaries.

We argue that an adequate understanding of human identity as a total social fact can be won only through an interpretation based on a social constructionist paradigm. On the other hand, we are not so foolish as to think that a total social fact is ever understood totally. Even less do we think that there is only one way to investigate social facts, and we have first-hand experience with the intrinsic limitation of any single study. No research study and perhaps no scholar can produce an adequate interpretation of identity. Nevertheless, the community of knowers is best served, we believe, by a social constructionist paradigm if the goal is deeper sociological psychological knowledge.

To clarify still further our theoretical allegiance, we distinguish two types of social constructionist strategies that we may label, we hope without offense, the reductionist and the pragmatic. *Reductionist* social constructionist thinkers tend to argue that there is no "reality" such as social structure; that individuals are responsible for their own identities; that imaginative and interactional processes exhaust the content of human meanings; that individual freedom is the touchstone of social reality; and that only certain evidences, empirical methods, and genres for presenting data are valid. *Pragmatic* social constructionist thinkers, on the other hand, tend to argue that there are irreducible "levels of social reality"; that individuals' responsibility for their own identities is variable and constrained; that imagination and interaction, as well as a priori social forms, enter and shape human meanings with variable but independent power; that individual freedom dialectically related to social determinism is the definitive social process; and that any communicable evidence, shared empirical methods, and interpretable genres for presenting data are valid, as long as – and here is the keystone – investigators are self-consciously in control of the relationships among data, questions, genre, assumptions, and the original social reality under investigation. Pragmatic social constructionist thinking, then, can be extended to include the work of other theoretical and empirical traditions, such as structural analysis, quantitative data, and hypothetico-deductive studies, whether from social surveys, experiments, or sociobiological research. The tough intellectual work is not simply to rule out methods or evidence a priori; rather, it is knowing how to interpret them meaningfully within an adequate theoretical paradigm. The task of Chapter 2 is to take a step, no matter how gingerly, toward these goals.

I. Identity:
its emergence within sociological
psychology

By the 1980s, *identity* has become a stock technical term in sociology and a widespread social label. Before the early 1940s, it was unknown. Within the span of about forty years, identity has become an indispensable technical term and a cultural buzzword. Its theoretical, empirical, and cultural importance shows no sign of abating as social scientists, clinicians, historians, psychologists, philosophers, and the media continue to apply, dispute, and develop the idea. Nevertheless, identity lacks an adequate theoretical development in contemporary sociological social psychology (cf. Rosenberg and Turner 1981).

The expanse of scholarly and popular writings on identity cannot, of course, be adequately handled in a single chapter. Nor is it our intent to do so. Rather, we focus on but one of the themes within the general issue of identity – namely, how this idea took shape and continues to thrive within the development of a sociological social psychology, or sociological psychology (see Weigert 1975). The presentation of material follows the chronological order of the seminal writings on identity. We focus the emergence of identity within sociological psychology around three questions:

1. What are the recent origins of the concept?
2. How did it find its way into sociological psychology?
3. Why was it so quickly taken over by sociological psychologists?

Accordingly, we attempt to locate the emergence of the term in its historical context, and to limn the main lines of development within sociological psychology.

Precursors to the concept of identity had been developing in the domains of sociology, anthropology, and psychology. The research and theorizing in these disciplines gave central importance to such concepts as self, character, and personality, respectively, through the period of World War II. The central paradigm informing these lines of development is summarized in the principle: *Social organization is the principle of self-organization, and both together explain social action.* Even into the early 1950s, sociologists (such as Riesman et al. 1950;

5

Gerth and Mills 1953/1964) conceptualized the social individual in terms of "character," probably accepting the importance of the term from anthropologists such as Benedict, Mead, and Kardiner. During this period, however, the term identity was incubating in the matrices of small groups of scholars concerned with interpreting American culture in the aftermath of World War II.

Historical and biographical moments in the emergence of identity

The plural origins and recent birth of American society had become a central focus in the two world wars. Twice within a single lifetime, Americans were mobilized to fight "over there" or to "remember Pearl Harbor." In neither war was there a popularly perceived direct threat that usually motives warfare, such as invasion, annexation, or loss of control of vital resources. American leaders, therefore, were deeply concerned with the problem of motivating a "nation of immigrants" to go to war against countries from which many of their own parents or grandparents had come. Men and women had to be persuaded that they were "Americans" as opposed to Germans, Italians, or Japanese, even if their names happened to be Hartmann, Cellino, or Toguchi. Nor were national leaders the only persons concerned. The everyday lives of people were touched by the same question, especially if a neighbor, teacher, or shopkeeper commented on a national origin from one of America's current enemies. Children whose parents spoke little or no English had to balance the tension between becoming 100 percent American and remaining loyal to the family. Such dilemmas in one form or another are the perennial problem of the immigrant. As a nation of immigrants recently at war with nations of origin, the problem became particularly intense for the United States.

In the late 1930s and through the period of World War II, a recent Viennese immigrant began a line of scholarly and literary productivity that gave birth to the concept of identity as a technical term. As a clinical psychoanalyst out of the Freudian tradition and specialized in the development and socialization of children, Erik Homburger Erikson brought a neo-Freudian schooling in the issue of children's identification with parents to his sensitive personal and clinical experience. He saw that children identify with parents over a wide range of deep human issues, such as existential security, sexuality, autonomy, shame, and guilt. Erikson was interested in the struggle children go through to synthesize the continual bodily changes of youth into a meaningful sense of an integrated ego capable of guiding them into a productive and secure adulthood.

True to his neo-Freudian heritage and clinical experience, Erikson studied the processes of ego synthesis in critical moments and under conditions of breakdown. Analysis of the abnormal and pathological enables the clinician to see the underlying normal processes at work more clearly. In addition, as an immigrant himself, Erikson experienced at first hand the process of acculturation into a new society under conditions of international tension and destructive warfare between his adopted country and his country of origin. A born and bred European scholar underwent the paradigmatic American experience of being an immigrant while already a mature adult and creative thinker.

The historical and personal reality of immigration was interpreted through Erikson's continual and vital dialogue with American psychoanalytic scholars. In addition, however, he began working with anthropologists and developing his methodological commitment to participation in and observation of the culture of those whose lives he was trying to understand. Erikson went into the field to understand how children develop a sense of ego synthesis, especially those children who are "in between" or struggling with unresolved ego crises. The anthropological experience gave the final impetus to Erikson's comparative analysis of ego development in anxious children. He studied American children in Vienna, arrogant Nazi youth, apathetic American Indians, confused war veterans, and crew members in submarines. He became acutely aware of the impact of historical reality and cultural change in the formation of youthful egos: How can a young Sioux Indian have a highly motivated and synthesized ego if the core cultural realities of buffalo hunter and warrior no longer exist? How can any youth shape a secure and synthesized ego if the socio-cultural context is ever-shifting and becoming more complex?

Erikson faced these questions both in his own life and in the people he studied. He took the polarity of human nature and social reality, interpreted it through the Freudian formulation of ethos and ego, and reformulated it as "group identity" and "ego identity" (Erikson 1946, 1956, reprinted 1959). His initial publications in which the term ego identity appears virtually coincide with the end of World War II. His reformulation of the human nature–social reality polarity introduced the new technical term he chose at least in part for its interdisciplinary usefulness (Erikson 1981). The term served prophetically to define a problem on which scholars from a wide range of disciplines, methodologies, theoretical orientations, and political leanings were to find common ground.

Erikson wrote virtually alone during the late 1940s and early 1950s about human development, historical change, and personal health, with identity as the organizing concept (cf. Fromm 1941). In his early formulations and consistent with his literary style, Erikson offered minimal definitional and theoretical elaboration. He distinguished routine "personal identity" as the normal way we are seen and interpreted by others from his technical use of ego identity. He gave *ego identity* a psychoanalytic and functional definition as a "group-psychological phenomenon.'' He wrote that "Ego identity . . . is the awareness of the fact that there is a selfsameness and continuity to the ego's synthesizing methods and that these methods are effective in safeguarding the sameness and continuity of one's meaning for others'' (1946, reprinted 1959: 23). Armed with this functional way of thinking, which is open to both psychological and sociohistorical reality, Erikson opened up a tremendous epistemological space for analyzing the human condition. He went on to write about inner identity, identity diffusion, wholeness and identity, racial group identities, psychosocial identity moratorium, psychohistory, and developmental identity over the life course.

In answer to a request for conceptual clarification, Erikson published the paradigmatic article, "The Problem of Ego Identity,'' in 1956. This treatment of ego identity is perhaps the single piece that has had the most influence on those working within sociological psychology. In it, he emphasizes that ego identity must be both a functioning psychological achievement of individuals and limited by, as well as fitted to, the sociohistorical moment in which that individual lives. He mentions the phrase "theory of identity'' toward the end of the article. He has indeed formulated a social psychoanalytic psychology. The key graphic in the article presents Erikson's eight-stage epigenesis of the person as he or she develops over the life course. Identity is the epigenetic task specific to adolescence, but Erikson sees contemporary society as essentially similar to the changing, ambivalent, uncertain environment of the adolescent. In effect, Erikson argues that contemporary society makes adolescents of us all, and thus identity crisis becomes the typical biographical crisis of the modern person.

The publication of his widely read and influential books, essays, and addresses fueled and solidified his impact. *Childhood and Society,* in which he especially thanks Margaret Mead, was published in 1950 and revised in 1963. Two key articles, including the paradigmatic piece, were reprinted in a single volume, *Identity and the Life Cycle* (1959, reissued 1980). Furthermore, his application of the concept of identity to Martin Luther (1958) gave a major impetus to the possibility of psychohistory as a synthesis of his theory of identity and historical analysis. His stream of publications continues the analysis of identity in the modern world, across cultures, and on into the later stages of the life cycle (Erikson 1968, 1968a, 1974, 1978; see Kakar 1979).

Erikson's conceptualization of identity combined his early developmental interest in the inner psychological unfolding of individual identity with his awareness of the impact of historical and sociocultural factors on the identities as they are realized. The paradigm of human nature–social reality is reformulated in the context of historical change and biographical circumstances into the powerful twins of identity-society and identity-history.

The diffusion of identity

The link between psychological reality and sociohistorical events proved attractive to sociologists working within the interactionist tradition of American pragmatism. One branch of this tradition was especially receptive. Following the coining of the phrase "symbolic interaction" by Herbert Blumer in the late 1930s, a group of scholars centered at the University of Chicago was developing, with a social nominalist and processual emphasis, the seminal ideas of George H. Mead concerning self and society (Lewis and Smith 1980). Erikson's work at Harvard influenced these Chicago symbolic interactionists, especially those interested in medical, psychiatric, and deviance issues.

An early and still influential publication fusing the two lines of thought is Nelson Foote's 1951 article in the *American Sociological Review*. Foote interpreted human motivation as a consequence of identification with a group. He conceptualized identification as the "appropriation of and commitment to a particular identity or series of identities. As a process, it proceeds by *naming:* its products are ever-evolving self-conceptions – with emphasis on the *con,* that is, upon ratification by significant others" [italics his]. Although he spends a paragraph indicating how much this idea owes to Freud and how it would differ from a Freudian explanation, Foote does not cite Erikson's work. Rather, he cites an intellectual debt to Mead's social behaviorism, and to an incipient social psychology with a symbolic interaction perspective indebted to literary sources such as Kenneth Burke. Indeed, Foote (1981) states that his reflections on identity were stimulated by his reading Erikson and earlier novels written during the 1930s.

In 1955 Foote coauthored *Identity and Interpersonal Competence,* dealing with family, personal competence, and public policy, with Leonard Cottrell, who followed a more behavioristic and situational interpretation of Mead's writings. Although the book featured identity in its title, the term is not defined or explicitly developed as an operative concept. Identity is simply described as a "wandering" thread that unites episodes, goes through dramatic changes, and is a central element in interpersonal competence and family life. The authors cite work done by social psychologists and social psychiatrists who share an emphasis on interpersonal relations and interaction as the matrix of human development. They cite Erikson's *Childhood and Society* approvingly in places, but without explicit recognition of, or dependence on, his attempts to formulate a definition of ego identity. Foote and his colleagues are part of a group of scholars from a variety of disciplines who share a discoverer's excitement over their common view of the "real" interactional process producing healthy human persons and of the central importance of a stable yet flexible self-conception or identity. They also share a normative interest, either as clinicians or policymakers.

Three years later, two more books appear that focus on identity. One by a psychoanalyst, Alan Wheelis, is entitled *The Quest for Identity* (1958). In spite of the title, the book primarily discusses character and superego, and uses identity "in its ordinary lay meaning" (p. 247). This lay usage is contrasted with the more precise meaning within psychoanalytic literature, at which point Wheelis refers to Erikson's 1956 paper on ego-identity. Apparently, in Wheelis's mind, identity is already a common lay term for making sense out of the crisis in the 1950s brought on by increasingly rapid social change and increased awareness of the changes (p. 84).

The second book, *On Shame and the Search for Identity* (1958, 1961), was written by the sociologist-philosopher Helen Merrell Lynd, coauthor of the famous *Middletown*. The book presents a tightly reasoned and wide-ranging discussion relating emotions, especially shame, to the issue of identity in postwar America. Like Wheelis, Lynd sees Americans as questing for a social psychological sense of well-being that has somehow been lost, and she uses the concept of identity as an analytical tool. Her heavily referenced argument relies on the writings of Erikson. Indeed, she begins her argument by summarizing Erikson's position, that "the search for identity has become as strategic in our time as the study of sexuality was in Freud's time" (Lynd 1961: 14). Lynd's creative argument synthesizes much of the writing on identity prior to 1958, including psychoanalytic, anthropological, psychological, sociological, linguistic, and historical sources. She includes page citations to work by Chicago sociologists – for example, to an unpublished mimeographed paper by Anselm Strauss, "An Essay on Identity" (University of Chicago 1957) – as well as to Erving Goffman's earlier essays. Her book serves as an important transition piece from psychoanalytic writings to work more central to sociological psychology.

The major impetus making identity a central concern for symbolic interactionists came from Strauss's published revision of his mimeographed essay. *Mirrors and Masks: The Search for Identity* was published in 1959 and recently reissued. In his preface, Strauss thanks a list of scholars, most of whom were connected at one time with the University of Chicago or Harvard University. The list includes virtually everyone who was to write a major piece on identity during the 1960s. A special note of thanks is given to Nelson Foote for his inspiration of the group project that motivated Strauss to write the essay (Strauss 1959, 1981). At the time, Strauss was working at the Psychosomatic and Psychiatric Institute in Chicago. He had earlier been at Indiana University and coauthored the classic symbolic interaction social psychology textbook with Alfred Lindesmith that has lasted for about forty years and five editions. True to classical symbolic interaction sources, however, the text speaks of self and not identity, except in a paragraph or two in later editions. Nevertheless, in his own book *Mirrors and Masks,* Strauss makes identity a technical term for sociological psychology. He sees identity as necessarily "connected with the fateful appraisals made of oneself – by oneself and by others" (p. 9).

The book's first citation is to Erikson's paradigmatic article, but it rejects the concept of ego-identity as an adequate definition for sociological psychology. Rather, Strauss follows the typical symbolic interaction procedure of using identity as a sensitizing concept, admittedly ambiguous and diffuse, in order to "better look around the corners of the problems, and be less likely to slide down the well-worn grooves of other men's thought" (pp. 9–10). He sees his task as fusing "symbolic interactional and social organizational perspectives into a workable, suggestive social psychology" (p. 11). Echoing the earlier article by Foote (1951), Strauss emphasizes language, naming, and interaction. Finally, he quotes Erikson's son, Kai Erikson, to the effect that Strauss is "discussing a facet of identity: that aspect of my subject which deals not with 'ego-identity' but with how persons become implicated with other persons and are affected, and affect each other, through that implication" (p. 13). These scholars are struggling for an adequate formulation of identity as an interactional reality. Strauss's incipient theory sees identity constituted by self-appraisals by self and others; by placements and evaluations of individuals; by names bestowed on persons; and by changes experienced and imposed over the course of a lifetime. His treatment served as a seminal text for symbolic interactionists, dramaturgical sociologists, and others working toward a sociological psychology.

A second modern classic for sociological psychology was published by a University of Chicago sociologist who shared many of Strauss's concerns, but who did not start with identity as a technical term. Erving Goffman's book, *The Presentation of Self in Everyday Life* (1959, earlier version published 1956), treats the definition and interpretation of individuals as performing characters in social situations. The entire essay is organized around the concept of self. Goffman concludes, against the commonsense view, that the "performed self" is a product of the interactional scene and not its cause.

Strauss's and Goffman's discussions reflect a continuing conceptual ambiguity indicated by the use of *self* and *identity* in similar analyses by exponents of a similar perspective, but without clear theoretical distinction. In this book, Goffman cites another influential University of Chicago sociologist, E. C. Hughes, whose work made passing use of the term identity (see Hughes 1971). The focus of Goffman's book is further sharpened by his familiarity with social psychiatry grounded in over a year of observational research at a large mental institution in Washington, D.C. This research provided a basis for his creative contribution to the study of identity, deviance, mental illness, and total institutions (Goffman 1961). Combined with his later work, Goffman's book on self in everyday life served as the principal piece for the dramaturgical stream within sociological psychology. Before leaving the 1950s, careful notice must be paid to a different direction aborning on the plains of Iowa. Manfred Kuhn is taken as the founder of the Iowa School of Meadian social psychology, in contrast to the Chicago School (Meltzer et al. 1975). He developed a quantitative and positivistic approach to the core issues of Meadian social psychology. Kuhn labeled his version of the Meadian paradigm that the organization of self reflects the organization of society, "self-theory." He introduced the widely used methodological tool, the Who Am I? or Twenty Statements test (TST) to generate data for testing propositions derived from self-theory.

In the TST, the respondent is asked to complete twenty statements in response to the question, Who am I? In a short, influential article, Kuhn and Thomas McPartland (1954) present the results of a modest but insightful study of college students' responses to the TST. The results are interpreted as adequately grasping the "self-attitudes" of the students, which in turn reflect their position in society and in their reference groups. The term identity is used in two important places in the article, but with no citation or elaboration, as though readers should know what it meant. Indeed, it reads like a synonym for the hyphenated Meadian derivation, self-attitude. In Kuhn's positivistic view, he concludes that "for prediction we need to have the *subjective* definitions of identity" (Kuhn and McPartland 1954: 76, their italics). In subsequent work, Kuhnian self-theory becomes nearly synonymous with the use of the TST, although some researchers simply adopt the language of identity (see Gecas et al. 1973). By the end of the 1950s, identity is widely used both technically and colloquially.

The reign of identity

The discussion of identity in the 1960s opens with a formidable book, *Identity and Anxiety* (Stein et al. 1960), edited by scholars in the New York area who took a critical stance toward American society. Although they introduce the collection of writings as concerned with identity in modern society, the only specific treatment of identity is the opening selection, Erikson's 1956 paper on ego identity. Nevertheless, the collection illustrates a rapidly emerging confluence of sociological, psychoanalytic, and existential writings into a broad-based critique of American mass society and its impact on meaning in individuals' lives. The topics of anxiety and alienation are linked to the issues of true and authentic versus false and pseudo identity. The concept also makes its entrance into the vocabulary of political scientists concerned with development and modernity (Pye 1960; see Mackenzie 1978).

The existential influence received continued articulation in the pages of the *Journal of the American Psychoanalytic Association,* the primary printed forum for the introduction of identity to the American scholarly community after the earlier pieces by Erikson. Beginning in 1963, Heinz Lichtenstein, who like Erikson was a European-trained psychoanalyst émigré, published a series of articles synthesizing sociological perspectives on identity, mainly the work of Riesman, Erikson, Strauss, and Lynd. Lichtenstein (1977) published a compilation of these and other writings on identity in a book organized around the idea of identity as an existential "dilemma," as a simultaneously and irreducibly private and public reality.

A small book by yet another European-trained scholar interpreting the American experience presented a reasonably systematic statement of the confluence of existential psychoanalysis and sociology on the modern "problematic" (problem context) of human identity. Hendrick Ruitenbeck's *The Individual and the Crowd: A Study of Identity in America* (1964) was but the second monograph on identity after Strauss's book. Ruitenbeck's treatment owes as much to existentialist philosophy as to psychoanalysis, with the sociology of mass society supplying the general historical context. Building on Erikson, Ruitenbeck sees identity as a needed integrative idea for making sense out of modern life, both analytically and existentially (p. 10). He closes his book with a call for continual self-reflection if individuals wish to sustain an authentic identity in modern society. The cultural use of identity is further indicated in a collection of addresses by religious thinkers that brought together traditional vocabulary such as "character," "self," and "soul" under the umbrella of a "search for identity" (Shinn 1964).

In 1965, a third monograph on identity was written by another European psychoanalyst, de Levita. This is an opaque and difficult mixture of exposition, neologism, and literary exercise aimed at furthering the initiatives of Erikson. Three years later, Erikson published his first book with identity in the title, *Identity: Youth and Crisis.* In this book, he maintains the clinical nuance, with emphasis on the "identity crisis" central to the problems of youth in advanced technological societies. The identity crisis is especially applicable to adolescence, that period of life that Erikson characterized by the developmental task of forming an integrated identity or suffering from the problem of identity diffusion. The book does not contribute further conceptual or theoretical development of identity, but it offers discussions of the identity of females, youth, and blacks. It clearly illustrates Erikson's blending of the analysis of pathological issues in human development with the interests of the clinician and the sensitivities of the social scientist.

In addition to continuing work in the psychoanalytic tradition, the 1960s saw the development of a powerful sociological psychology of identity from two sources: the continuation of symbolic interactionist work from the Foote–Strauss formulations; and the emergence of a mostly independent perspective from classical sociological writers and European social phenomenology in the work of Peter Berger and Thomas Luckmann, émigré scholars schooled together at the New School for Social Research in classical theory and in the teaching of Alfred Schutz. Furthermore, the psychologist Edgar Schein (1961, republished 1971) offered a sketch and application of identity theory in his attempt to explain the phenomenon of brainwashing. Momentum was building on a variety of fronts.

In the early 1960s, two influential statements from the symbolic interaction perspective were written by scholars mentioned in Strauss's preface to *Mirrors and Masks*. "Appearance and the Self," an essay by Gregory P. Stone (1962), a Chicago-trained sociologist who taught for many years at the University of Minnesota, appeared in the first anthology of symbolic interaction social psychology. Although Stone uses "self" in the title, he explicitly recognizes Erikson for introducing identity into social science. Stone goes on to offer the first concise definition of identity widely used within sociological psychology. Identity is a meaning that a self acquires when *"situated* – that is, cast in the shape of a social object by the acknowledgement of his participation or membership in social relations" (Stone 1962: 93; italics his). Furthermore, identity is continuously changing, since it *"is intrinsically associated with all the joinings and departures of social life"* (p. 94; italics his).

Identity places and evaluates a person according to the structural values and interpersonal mood realized in the situation. Stone picks up the themes of Erikson, Strauss, Goffman, and Lynd, and takes them a theoretical step further by explicitly linking identity to situated social relationships, while distinguishing the dimensions of cognition, evaluation, and emotion. In addition, he makes a key empirical and theoretical contribution by discussing "appearances" as the situational foundation for the identities that persons present to others and have bestowed on themselves.

The theme of appearances and identity underlies another important book by Erving Goffman that explicitly deals with identity, *Stigma: Notes on the Management of Spoiled Identity* (1963). This book continues his analysis of the meanings of self-in-situations and applies the analysis to those who must present or attempt to hide a stigmatized self. The essay is developed in terms of identity, which Goffman distinguishes into three kinds: social, personal, and ego, in that order. He begins by describing the entrance of a stranger and the process of interpreting appearances that "enable us to anticipate his category and attributes, his 'social identity' – to use a term that is better than 'social status' because personal attributes such as 'honesty' are involved, as well as structural ones, like 'occupation' " (p. 2). Without citation or explanation, Goffman uses the phrase "social identity" throughout the book with nothing more than this simple justification based on an apparent commonsense understanding and the distinction between personal and structural attributes. With this distinction, he is able to give a powerful and general sociological psychological definition of *stigma* as "a special kind of relationship between attribute and stereotype" (p. 4). So defined, stigma can be investigated across the range of such relationships and can serve as a creative perspective on the sociology of deviance, as Goffman uses it in his last chapter.

Personal identity, by contrast with social identity, is described as "positive marks or identity pegs, and the unique combination of life history items that comes to be attached to the individual with the help of these pegs for his identity" (p. 57). He goes on to add: "What is difficult to appreciate is that personal identity can and does play a structured, routine, standardized role *[sic]* in social organization just because of its one-of-a-kind quality." Unlike the naked introduction of social identity, Goffman bolsters the idea of personal identity with a few citations. He refers to psychoanalytic literature and a volume published in England that he uses mainly in the context of proving identity by legally accepted ways, such as identity papers. Personal identity results from the combination of bodily markers and biographical detail, and Goffman thanks Harold Garfinkel for introducing him to the idea of biography as he uses it (p. 62).

Finally, Goffman sees "ego or felt" identity as coming from psychoanalytic work, Erikson's by name, though without citation. Ego-identity, however, is not used here in the fully technical psychoanalytic sense; indeed, Goffman notes that he would have preferred the term "self-identity." *Ego* or *felt* identity refers to "the subjective sense of his own situation and his own continuity and character that an individual comes to obtain as a result of his various social experiences" (p. 105). Thus, Goffman sees ego-identity as the sense of existential continuity resulting from social experiences. Even the most subjective dimension of identity becomes subject matter for a sociological psychology.

Goffman's tentative but sensitive conceptualizations of the three kinds of identity allow him to interpret the individual in relation to cultural stereotypes historically available for constituting social identity; to analyze interactional processes of information control and the management of discrediting information in the situational maintenance of a creditable personal identity; and to relate both kinds of identity to that which is appropriated and "felt" by the individual as making up the existential ego or self. This presentation parallels Mead's classical treatment of the trilogy of society–self–mind, and brings many of the theoretical strands of identity analysis to bear on a single theme – stigma – with the fruitful result that it illuminates how individuals are constituted as deviant, on the one side, and how normals are sustained in their normalcy, on the other. Goffman is heavily influenced by psychiatric writings about identity. His work also begins to show the influence of Alfred Schutz's social phenomenology through such ideas as biography or unthinking routines – ideas apparently channeled through personal communication with Harold Garfinkel (see pp. 62, 88; see Goffman 1961a).

In the same year that *Stigma* appeared, Peter Berger published *Invitation to Sociology,* a widely read introductory book that features the idea of biography. Without mentioning Erikson, Berger sprinkles the book with discussions of identity in relation to role theory and the construction and reconstruction of biographical meaning. There is no explicit attempt to justify or develop the idea of identity. Rather, Berger assumes that the term is reasonably familiar and uses it to perform a piece of theoretical alchemy: He attributes the origins of a theory of identity to the classical writings of Charles H. Cooley and George H. Mead, both of whom, however, speak of self. In the development of his own version of role theory that integrates European sociology of knowledge with the micro, interactional emphasis of American sociological psychology, Berger finds the term identity more appropriate and simply appears to put it into the mouths of his sources. He does cite Strauss, but we found no reference to Erikson's work.

In his discussion of personal change, Berger analyzes adult conversion and contrasts it with "alternation," a kind of identity mobility that he sees as characteristic of and highly functional in modern society. His conceptualization of identity is derived from the classic writings of Durkheim, Marx, Simmel, and Weber, and synthesized around the social phenomenological perspective of Schutz (see 1962, 1967). Berger develops his version of role theory and social types and combines it with Goffman's dramaturgy, which he acknowledges explicitly. Underlying the book is an incipient version of the microsociology of everyday knowledge that he is in the process of developing with Thomas Luckmann.

In the following four years, Berger and Luckmann produced an impressive series of publications presenting a theoretical perspective that is for the most part independent of the psychoanalytic literature on identity, although Berger (1981) remarks that the term identity itself may have come from Erikson's influence. The issue of personal identity construction and maintenance in relation to social processes is treated in an article that lays out the historical context of a socially and psychologically mobile society in which identity becomes a problem for people on the move (Luckmann and Berger, 1964). They speak of a "sociological perspective on identity from the work of Cooley and Mead which makes clear the basis for the 'crisis of identity' facing modern persons" (p. 335). They cite Strauss's book; the book of readings compiled by Stein et al., especially the introductory essay; and Riesman's *The Lonely Crowd,* a most influential book in this line of thought.

That same year, Berger and Hansfried Kellner, a European with a doctorate in sociology from The New School, published another widely cited article on the "construction of reality" within marriage (1964). Again, they speak of a "Meadian perspective on identity" as a source of their thesis that marriage is a strenuous exercise in the construction of a common and precarious reality between two previous strangers (p. 2). The theoretical section of the paper relies almost entirely on European sources generally focused on philosophical anthropology. Personal identity and biography are discussed almost as taken-for-granted ideas within the context of marriage. This taken-for-granted status of identity continues in Berger's article, "Identity as a Problem in the Sociology of Knowledge" (1966), which contains a preliminary synthesis of a Meadian "dialectic of socialization" that constitutes the self, a process Berger translates into a problem in the sociology of knowledge from European sources without any definition of or citation for identity. Berger simply asserts: *"One identifies oneself, as one is is identified by others, by being located in a common world"* (p. 111, italics his), and without settling the ultimate epistemological issue, every common world is constructed through the social dialectics that make up human life. Berger sees the dialectical processes as the fundamental propositions for both Meadian and sociology of knowledge perspectives, and as providing the basis for a "sociological psychology" (p. 110), a concern similar to but independent of Strauss's – namely, to generate a sociological perspective on human self-understanding.

The preliminary synthesis of sociology of knowledge, Meadian social psychology, and classical sociological writings receives a fuller statement in the short but paradigmatic book that gave the name to this emerging perspective, Berger and Luckmann's *The Social Construction of Reality* (1966). Within the framework of the social construction of human reality, identity is conceptualized as a social meaning constructed like other meanings, *but* with the uniquely existential dimension of being anchored in an individual's body. There is a particularly human dialectic involved in the construction of identity – namely the dialectic of the individual's body and the social meanings existing outside that body. Historically available *types* of identity are purely social realities; indeed, they are nothing but social. Actual personal identity, on the other hand, is a social reality vivified in individual experience and anchored in individual bodies. There is a dual dialectic generating the complete reality of human identity: the total social reality of identity types dialectically related to unique personal identity; and personal identity dialectically related to the irreducibly physical reality of the body (pp. 150ff). The organism will out!

Both Berger and Luckmann continue these reflections in their differing interpretations of religion. Berger's book, *The Sacred Canopy* (1967), applies a substantive definition of religion as a "sacred cosmos" that bestows the ultimately valid identity on humans: the name by which they are known by God. Luckmann, on the other hand, presents a reductively functional argument that religion is any symbolic form by which humans transcend organic life, as implied in the English title of his book, *The Invisible Religion* (1967; an earlier version was published in German in 1963).

Also in 1966, a fourth monograph on identity was published. Two scholars from the symbolic interaction tradition explicitly link role theory and interactionism in an analytic and taxonomic treatment of identity. George McCall and J. L. Simmons' book, *Identities and Interactions* (1966), builds on the first author's continuing interest in human self-understanding and its empirical study. The book is indebted to the empirical tradition of Kuhn, as the authors attest in their opening sentence, but it shows sensitivity to the work of Goffman and other structural interpreters of symbolic interactionism, sans mention of Herbert Blumer. The work of Erikson is briefly cited in a mention of identity in adolescence.

McCall–Simmons state their main focus: The central concept of the book is labeled "role-identity" which is "the character and the role that an individual devises for himself as an occupant of a particular social position" (p. 67). They rely on Strauss (1959) and Goffman (1959, 1963) for their understanding of identity as both social and personal. In a final chapter setting forth a mainline positivistic research agenda, they operationalize role-identity by the Who Am I? or Twenty Statements test. They use concepts from exchange theory such as investment, and from role theory such as coherence, salience, and prominence. These concepts allow an elaboration of role-identity located within the life trajectory and overlapping careers. It offers a suggestive synthesis and holds promise for a positivistic research enterprise.

The original book was translated into German. In 1978, a revision was published that differed little from the first version except for a new preface documenting intervening developments, and the addition of the interesting subtitle, "An Examination of Human Associations in Everyday Life," attesting to the emergence of everyday life as an important theme during the 1970s (see Douglas et al. 1980; Weigert 1981). They note also that "One of the most striking trends of the decade has been the adoption of concepts of *identity*" (p. xii, italics theirs).

Along with the work of Strauss and Berger and Luckmann, *Identities and Interactions* ranks as an important systematic statement heralding a viable sociological psychology with identity as a central organizing idea without relying on Erikson's psychoanalytic perspective. The mainstreams of classical sociological thought, American social behaviorism, and more recent social phenomenology have come together into a powerful perspective on identity. The TST and other survey instruments provide data for the development of a positivistic tradition of research, and participant observation does the same for more qualitatively oriented traditions (see Stryker 1968; Becker et al. 1961). The foundation is fully laid by the end of the 1960s. Now a sociological psychology of identity is ready to address the normative and clinical issues, such as normal and deviant social identity.

Two rather brief functional statements published at this time strengthened the place of identity in a general theory of society and religion. Talcott Parsons (1968) found the concept a useful addition to his action theory. Identity, he reasoned, has become a "fashionable term" in contemporary society because of the increasing structural differentiation of society, resulting in the pluralization of role-involvements. This complexity presents a wide range of possible choices and subsequent cross-pressures once the individual makes a commitment to one or another set of positions and acquires the attendant identities (p. 11). The modern person is much more aware of the problem of identity than persons living in simpler, stabler societies. Faced with this historical condition, social theorists may profitably use identity as a technical term to designate "the *core system of meanings of an individual personality* in the mode of *object* in the interaction system of which he is part" (p. 14, italics his). In the article, Parsons relies on his earlier formulations of action theory and the psychoanalytic tradition, with but one passing reference to Erikson.

Robert Bellah published a sociological analysis of identity alongside that by Erikson in the *International Encyclopedia of the Social Sciences* (1968). (Identity was not even an entry in the earlier *Encyclopedia of the Social Sciences* published in 1934.) Bellah presents a simple and concise argument for the theoretical relationship between religion and identity: Human identity is a necessary and universal function of religion. This functional argument develops the observation of Berger that the surest name an individual has is the one given by God. Bellah builds on the foundation of a Durkheimian theory of the reality of individual existence rendered meaningful by the symbolic categories of collective life.

The twin themes of normalcy and deviance are developed at a generalized societal level and conceptualized in sociological terms partly by Erikson's previously mentioned *Identity: Youth and Crisis* (1968), and explicitly by two books published the following year by West Coast scholars. Orrin Klapp's book, *Collective Search for Identity* (1969), tried to make sense out of the youth movements and student unrest of the 1960s. Klapp interpreted post–World War II America as bent in an overly bureaucratic and discursively rational direction. He echoes the "loss of community" theme of radical critics of modern society. In building his analysis, Klapp explicitly relies on Erikson, Strauss, Stone, Goffman, and his own earlier work on social types for unpacking the idea of identity.

Combined with work from the perspective of collective behavior and social movements, Klapp interprets the youth movements of the 1960s as a largely ineffective searching for a symbolically and emotionally effective collective identity based on nondiscursive, nonrational meanings. He argues that collective responses to social conditions indicate that basic social institutions no longer satisfy the inherent human need for a stable, continuous, and meaningful identity produced by the totally social means of symbols, interactions, and social types (pp. 5–6). He sees the need for identity as "a need for a socially confirmed concept of self (adequate ego symbolism); fullness of sentiments, including mystiques; and centering or devotion, so that a person's life is focused on a point where he recognizes some highest value" (p. ix). Once individuals feel the need for identity, they are motivated to engage in a search for it. If the need results from institutional failure to supply meaning, then the search becomes collective and *"outside the organizational and institutional channels"* (p. ix, italics his). This treatment extends the use of identity by synthesizing it with collective behavior that is largely extrainstitutional, just as Berger–Luckmann and McCall–Simmons synthesized identity with role theory within interpretive and institutional contexts, respectively.

The second book published in 1969 constructs a conceptual framework and taxonomic treatment of identity in relationship to the other domain of human conduct that is negatively defined, yet dialectically constituted by, institutional meanings – namely, deviance. John Lofland's *Deviance and Identity* builds on the symbolic interactional and classical sociological conceptualizations of identity. Lofland's contribution is to apply identity to the area of deviance, which at that time was a fruitful area in sociological theory and a hotbed for the continued growth of a sociological psychology. He constructs a conceptual framework for deviance as the acquisition of consistent, long-lasting, and intense "deviant identities" that are assumed to define the essence of the person. Such analysis sensitizes us to the labels, agencies, processes, and consequences of imposing or acquiring a deviant identity.

More deeply, Lofland notes that the analysis of deviant identities pays great dividends through an increased awareness of the conflicts and paradoxes at the moral core of the human condition. He concludes that achievement-oriented societies are characterized by ambivalent "kinds of paradoxical mischief created by social categories [that] are, then, among the mischievous ironies implicit in the study of deviant identities and identities more generally" (p. 307). Thus, the study of deviant identities leads to a general theory of human identity analogous to the insight gained by Goffman's (1963) analysis of stigma as a "deviantizing" relationship between a social stereotype and a personal attribute. A third book published in the same year (Chickering 1969) linked education with identity in the title, but with no technical use of the concept to further its development.

At this point, a general sociological–psychological perspective on identity is framed and ready for application in the 1970s, although many leading symbolic interactionists were still using self as an "indispensable concept" with no strong mention of identity (Melzer et al. 1975: 116–17). A series of important articles, however, traces such relevant issues as mutual identity awareness and bestowal; adapting to life as performance; and sustaining normalcy by verbal accounts (Messinger et al. 1962; Weinstein and Deutschberger 1963; Glaser and Strauss 1964; Scott and Lyman 1968).

The application and theoretical articulation of identity

By the dawn of the 1970s, identity was sufficiently formulated and accepted as both a technical and a folk category that scholars could use the term without challenge and with easily shared assumptions about its legitimacy and importance. A popular book by a psychoanalyst went so far as to characterize American society, and by implication any modern society, as an "identity society" (Glassner 1972). Identity has become a cultural cliché; the meaning of the term is superseded by its function of nominally explaining the dynamics of life's meaning (cf. Zijderveld 1979). Simultaneously, philosophers return to the age-old question of the possibility and conditions of personal identity as a philosophical problem, admitting of no certain or clear answer even though it remains one of the most unshakable certainties in everyday experience (see the writings collected in Perry, 1975; Rorty, 1976). Within the broad parameters of identity both as the object of sharp philosophical analysis and as a cultural cliché for making sense out of everyday experience, sociological psychology research and theoretical articulation accelerate across a wide range of applications at both the micro, interactional and the macro, institutional levels.

Micro analyses

At the interactional level, sociological psychologists pursued a variety of methods to study the presence, function, and change in multiple identities across cognitive, affective, and behavioral domains. The work of Sheldon Stryker moved strongly toward this goal in the years since his brief 1968 paper on identities and roles in family research. Toward the end of the 1970s, he and his colleagues organized a trainee program in social psychology at Indiana University in which the issue of identity played a central part. Stryker (1977) labels this approach "identity theory" within the symbolic interaction tradition.

Identity theory is directly related to the role-identity model of McCall–Simmons. Stryker offers a propositional summary of identity theory that builds on the paradigmatic principle of the self and society relationship stated at the beginning of this chapter, on a structural model of society, and on quantitative methods of doing science (1968, 1977, 1980; Stryker and Serpe 1982). This version of identity theory is a "structural interactionism" and offers bridging links to other streams of social psychology sensitive to sociological concerns, such as attribution theory and ethnomethodology (see Guiot 1977; Hadden and Lester 1978).

The idea of role-identity continued to be developed by those who used computer applications to analyze data generated by the TST procedure (Gordon, 1968, 1976). Furthermore, a colleague of Stryker, Peter Burke, used the semantic differential as a visual as well as analytical tool for articulating and testing propositions derived from identity theory. Although he uses the language of self, Burke (1980) talks mainly about identity and role-identity as the measurable components of self. Burke insists that the two requisites of measurement techniques are that they be "theoretically grounded and . . . quantitative" (1980: 18). He finds the semantic differential method meeting these requisites and offering a way for the theoretical work of symbolic interactionists to be used by quantitative social psychologists.

Burke conceptualizes identity as the subjective component of role. Interrelated multiple role-identities constitute self. The issues of hierarchies of multiple identities, their relative salience within the hierarchies, the differential commitment of individuals to the variously ranked identities, and all this related to situational behavior and social structure emerge as central empirical questions for identity theory. An analogous development in the experimental study of "situated identities" brings together attribution theory and the situational emphasis of symbolic interactionism (see Alexander and Wiley 1981). Together, these lines of analysis constitute quantitative research agendas in the positivistic, theory-building mode that cuts across current boundaries of the varieties of social psychologies with identity providing the cutting edge.

During the 1970s, another domain of interactional identity served as a kind of *experimentum crucis* for the thesis of the social construction of identity. If there is any identity that seems to be given with physical existence and not reducible to societal definitions, it is the identity of male or female. Yet the logical implication of the ethnomethodological and social constructionist approaches is that identities emerge from and are realized in interaction like all human meanings. Sociological psychologists make the point by distinguishing sex, which is biologically derived, from gender, which is socially and psychologically derived (see Gagnon and Simon, 1973; Walum, 1977).

At the same time that a sociological–psychological understanding of gender identity was being formulated, medical technology, surgical practice, and hormonal options made a postoperative transsexual a physical possibility for the first time in history. Knowledge of the process of becoming a complete transsexual deepened appreciation of the social processes and artful practices by which all identities, ordinary or extraordinary, are constructed and realized (see Garfinkel 1967: 116–85, 285–8; Kessler and McKenna 1978; and Morris 1975, for a literate version). The same generic social and psychological processes are assumed to be working in the interactional realization of these cases, as in normal, mundane identity construction. These "deviant" cases, then, are like crucial experiments laying bare the underlying structural features and interactional processes that provide meaningful identities in the taken-for-granted world in which impressions are continuously managed and identities must be bargained (Blumstein 1973; Schlenker 1980).

Studies of homosexuals demonstrate the dialectical relationship between social types and personal attributes. Persons who are physically "normal" but who have sexual preferences and life-styles that are not socially defined as normal according to the cultural code of the heterosexual assumption illustrate identity construction and maintenance. The subtle dynamics of passing, or appearing "authentic" in a presented identity that is negated by one's "real" identity, is the constant achievement of covert but active homosexuals. The more public dynamics of community building and cultural change are the tasks faced by overt and organizationally active homosexuals (see Ponse 1978; Warren 1974).

Institutional analyses

At the next level of social organization, there is a plethora of institutional identities that link individuals to mediating social structures. There is occupational identity, legal identity, educational identity, neighborhood identity, family identity, and so on. These are the institutional identities that fill out our identity experience (Gordon 1976). In modern society, many of these identities are recorded in our identity "kit" and linked fatefully to each of us by name, number, rank, or title.

Many studies of groups and categories of persons used the idea of identity as an organizing concept. Ethnicity, above all, emerged as a central and hot issue during the 1960s and continues into the 1980s. The phrase "ethnic identity" quickly became a cause for national policy as well as an issue for self-definition and defense (Glazer and Moynihan, 1975; Gleason, 1983). Scholars debated whether ethnic identity is somehow a given, "primordial" reality, or something that can be realized strategically and circumstantially. Building on his work concerning Jewish identity, Dashefsky (1976) brings together a representative set of papers concerned with the general issue of individual identification with a socially recognized group. The framework for the book gently synthesizes the main lines of thought we have presented from Erikson, the qualitative orientation of Strauss and Goffman, and the quantitative tradition.

The civil rights and other movements brought racial, ethnic, and minority identities to the forefront of national consciousness and political action, as well as into the pages of social scientific analysis. In the political context of growing ethnic awareness, apologists, intellectuals, and politicians re-asked questions analogous to the earlier ones of natural character or personality type – namely, is there an American identity? The assimilationists, pluralists, and separatists give their irreconcilable answers, yet Americans go on with some sense of being different from other peoples (Mann 1979).

Institutional analysis continued in the study of religion. In *Identity and the Sacred,* Hans Mol (1976) argues that identity formation and maintenance is the central function of religion. This argument picks up the theme emphasized by Bellah, who applied his understanding of religion and identity in analyses of religion in America, both civil and sacred (1970, 1975). Scholars used Mol's formulation to interpret the relationship between identity and religion in a variety of contemporary societies (1978). This line of reflection takes the identity–religion link beyond the context of modernized and "mass" societies like the United States, and argues that religion serves the essential function of stabilizing individual identity in any society. Echoing Berger (1967), Mol defines religion as *"sacralization of identity"* (p. 1, italics his). Thus identity becomes the core problem in a theoretical understanding of religion. Indeed, identity emerges as a central and seemingly quasi-religious theme in modern literature (Langbaum 1977), and offers a perspective for interpreting the link between city life and puritanism (Sennett 1971).

Macro societal analysis reached a general theoretical level in the essays elaborating societal or cross-cultural analyses along the lines of Mol's identity and religion, or Erikson's identity and adulthood in India (Kakar 1979). We now come full circle from the "culture and personality" analysis that preceded the emergence of identity. Instead of terms like personality, character, or self, however, *identity* is the central organizing concept. Presumably, scholars now find the term analytically developed, reasonably value-neutral, and paradigmatically adequate.

Special note must be made of Erikson's continued influence as he takes his concern for identity into the later stages of the life course and stimulates scholars from other societies to do the same. His work now spans the four decades during which identity emerged as both an analytic term and a cultural cliché. In his writing and lecturing, he analyzed identity in childhood, adolescence, and now adulthood; in individual biographies; in both group and societal histories; and in traditional and contemporary settings (see Erikson 1983). Throughout his writings, the pervasive clinical concern, avowed normative and moral interests, and consistent functional reasoning are couched in a learned, elegant, yet clear and engaging style of presentation that lends credence to this insistence that the unity and continuity of identity is the characteristic social psychological issue of our times.

Macro analyses

Toward the middle of the 1970s, another theoretical perspective on identity, partially independent of those we have discussed, came from the critical theory of Jürgen Habermas. Working mainly from the inspiration of the critical theorists of the Frankfurt School who tried to integrate Freud and Marx, Habermas (1974) strove to formulate a theoretical version of social evolution and personal development based on underlying homologies between the two processes. He sees social identity evolving from primitive mythic and kinship foundations to contemporary rational and communicative relationships. Within this overall scheme, he tries to integrate contemporary psychoanalytic, sociological, and developmental psychology perspectives on individual identity into a synthetic and normative argument for a sense of identity based on communicative competence, rationality, and tolerance – a universal pragmatics (1979). Habermas offers a historically grounded perspective with an emancipatory interest and normative thrust for analyzing identity.

Development of general sociological theory is the clear purpose pervading the essays published by Roland Robertson and Burkart Holzner, *Identity and Authority: Exploration in the Theory of Society* (1979). The essays reflect another and partially independent tradition of scholarship – namely, comparative civilizational analysis. The authors depend somewhat on psychoanalytic, symbolic interactional, and sociology of knowledge traditions. They rely more heavily, however, on classical sociological theory and the macro-level formulations of functionalists such as Parsons, with explicit recognition of the relevance of Habermas's critical theory. The essays treat the macro issues of societal evolution and invariance, modernization of society and self, and in general the key link between modes of authority and codes of identity. Authority has traditionally been a central issue in theories of society. The goal of these authors is to make identity a central concern as well. With these essays, the problematic of identity has taken a center-stage position in social theory at the general macro level.

A map of identity's emergence and a summary

The discussion thus far traces the main lines along which identity has emerged as a technical term within sociological psychology. Figure 1.1 presents a summary of the discussion in which we discern five partially independent lines of

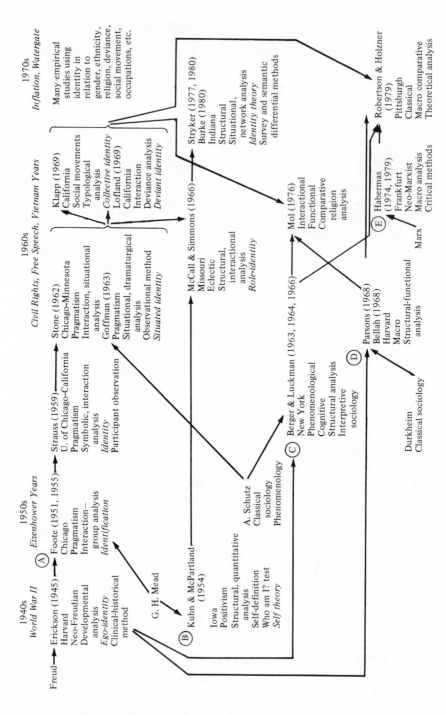

Figure 1.1 Main lines of the emergence of identity in sociological social psychology.

emergence marked by the capital letters A–E across the roughly forty years from Erikson's initial formulations of ego identity in the 1940s. Under each major figure, we indicate the predominant institutional affiliation; the central theoretical orientation in that line of thought; the term or phrase characteristic of that body of writings; and where it seemed appropriate, the particular methodological stance used by scholars working in the perspective. Erikson, for example, worked mainly at Harvard University out of a neo-Freudian and developmental theoretical perspective and started our story by coining the term ego-identity for his clinical-historical interpretations.

Erikson's work directly influenced Nelson Foote and Anselm Strauss in the symbolic interaction line that grew out of the work of George H. Mead at Chicago and moved to the San Francisco–Berkeley area. This line of thought worked from American pragmatism, focused on interaction among individuals and within groups through participant observation methods, and spoke of identification and identity. By contrast, a second line of emergence from the work of Mead started at the University of Iowa within a positivistic operationalism that sought structural relationships and quantitative data concerning self-definitions or using their own instrument, the TST, to develop self theory. The rest of the figure can be read in similar fashion, so that we see five partially independent lines of emergence, each indebted to different seminal thinkers or clusters of thinkers and recognized theoretical perspectives: Freud and psychoanalysis; G. H. Mead and symbolic interactionism; Alfred Schutz, along with selected aspects of classical and interpretive sociology; Durkheim, with aspects of classical and structural-functional sociology; and finally, Marx and critical theory.

At the beginning of the 1980s, there appears to be a dual convergence of theoretical perspectives on identity as a fully accepted technical term. At the micro, interactional level, identity is seen as multiple categorizations of the individual by both self and others that vary by situation, influence behavior, and constitute life's meanings. This convergence is shared by all sociological psychologists, if we may risk an empirical generalization to the best of our knowledge. Methodologically, however, there are two distinct traditions: One is qualitative and interpretationist, relying on participation and observation; the other is quantitative and causal, relying on questionnaires, experiments, and measurement. These two methodological styles reflect the division between the Chicago and Iowa schools of symbolic interactionism mentioned above. Both agree, however, that identity is a key concept for sociological psychology.

The second convergence is the macro, systemic level. Identity is conceptualized as a systemic problematic that must be reasonably resolved for a healthy social order. Identity is a positional definition of actors within institutions and societies. Macro analysts, then, tend to see identity as an a priori structural aspect of institutions such as religion, occupation, education, family, and so on, or as a deeper cultural code of personal meanings that relate the individual to the most general level of societal meanings. The split between institutional and societal analysts seems more a division of labor than the result of any methodological differences, although the societal analysts incline to larger historical questions of social evolution and the comparative dynamics of entire civilizations. Both types of analysis share a common conviction of the importance of identity as a key term for contemporary social theory.

Overlapping the divergence of theories of identity into micro and macro analyses is its potential usefulness as a bridging concept for analysis that cuts across all levels. This is a promise only the future work of the community of theorists and researchers can fulfil. The fruitful link with psychoanalytic and historical work may again propel deeper understanding of contemporary society as the consulting rooms of America echo with talk of a weak and wilted self seeking love in narcissism (Lasch 1978). Work with the Who Am I? test suggests a self-consciousness that is more reflective, complex, and ''mutable'' as a coping style adaptive to contemporary society (Zurcher 1977). Scholars concerned with traditional values such as loyalty and love argue that identity is found in sacrifice and commitment, not in going with the flow (Kilpatrick 1975). Even analysis of contemporary nostalgia finds the yearning for a stable and continuous identity to be a key interpretive component (Davis 1979). On the other hand, identity-seeking may lead to ''escape attempts'' from an everyday life seen as a prison (Cohen and Taylor 1978). Whether such clinical, normative, and historical analyses can be persuasively integrated with the observational and experimental work of symbolic interactionists and attribution theorists remains to be seen, but such deeper convergence is not ruled out a priori. Promising recent empirical work analyzes apartheid (du Preez 1980), threatened identities (Breakwell 1983), social isolation (Thoits 1983), housing and the environment (Duncan 1982), and continues research on ethnicity through a variety of methodologies (Gumperz 1982; Tajfel 1982).

As we come to the end of our story of the emergence of identity as a technical term in sociological psychology, we see outlines of answers to the questions Why identity? and Why identity now? The preparadigmatic understanding of a kind of parallel between social organization and self-organization in children's identification with adults already underlay sociologically oriented social psychology in the interwar period of the 1920s and 1930s. The great upheaval of World War II presented a historical context in which the question of what it means to be an American, German, French, Italian, Russian, or Japanese came to the forefront of consciousness. Finally, an individual whose biography bridged Europe and America and psychoanalysis and social science struggled to make sense out of children's development in different cultures. Erikson was led by his own reflection to coin the phrase "ego identity" and to develop identity as the best term for interdisciplinary use.

This reasonably value-neutral and interdisciplinary term was quickly picked up by those interested in Erikson's work or sharing his therapeutic concern for the socialization of children, as well as by others radically critical of malaise among middle-class adults in so-called mass industrial society. With the spread of social conflict attending the rise of civil rights and countercultural movements, the language of identity was generalized from clinical, familial, or radical contexts, and used positively by groups to legitimize their own claims to social and legal recognition. Identity was translated into normal, social, and historical contexts demanding the attention of every discipline concerned with grasping the meaning of individual and group existence in today's world.

The widespread acceptance of the concept of identity does not imply agreement on or even a clear understanding of its various meanings (Gleason 1983). The lines of emergence discussed in this chapter leave us with a set of dialectical relationships tensely coexisting within the conceptualizations of identity: stability and change; subjective, objective, and intersubjective; individual, group, and sociocultural; cognitive, affective, and behavioral; conscious and unconscious; situationally specific versus transsituationally generic; continuous development and transformation versus discontinuous rupture and crisis; situationally emergent or contextually determined (see Mackenzie 1978; Wilshire 1982). Obviously, we cannot resolve or even adequately treat these dialectical relationships of identity. Nevertheless, the following chapters attempt to codify, apply, and speculatively to extend our understanding of identity as a key concept for a sociological psychology adequate to today's world. The theoretical centrality of identity derives from the realization that identity is a contemporary rendition of the perennial issue: How are we to understand the definition of a human person in such a way as to gain a deeper understanding of our selves and our times? This realization motivates the chapters that follow.

2. Sociological psychology and identity theory:
a propositional essay

In Chapter 1, we traced the emergence of identity as a central concept in socio-logical social psychology. Although its authoritative history is yet to be written, the concept clearly arises from the work of Erik Erikson. From there, it spread as a technical, clinical, and folk term. To scholars working in the symbolic interaction tradition within sociology, it showed promise of significant analytic power. Yet as one of these scholars, Anselm Strauss, noted in the opening line of his influential work *Mirrors and Masks* (1959, reissued 1971), "Identity as a concept is fully as elusive as is everyone's sense of his own personal identity." The first chapter tried to diminish that elusiveness somewhat.

The seminal question

The human quest to answer the seminal question, What is a human being that we are mindful of ourselves and of one another? demands constant attention. Thinkers try to answer the question from the symbols historically available to them. Traditionally, answers came from mythical, religious, theological, hu-manistic, philosophical, and everyday world views. In the past century, the rise of psychological and social sciences provided yet other symbols and models for addressing this question. After World War II, the English-speaking world for-mulated the seminal question in terms of individual identity from the psycholog-ical tradition, and social identity from the sociological tradition. "Identity" be-came the translation of this era's answer to the seminal question.

Although identity emerged as a concept that spans psychological, sociologi-cal, historical, theological, and philosophical disciplines, this chapter focuses on human identity as a construct within a sociological social psychology. We see identity as a social reality; indeed, as a social reality that is continually produced within and by the experience and interaction of individuals (Berger and Luck-mann 1966; Schutz and Luckmann 1973). The specific object of analysis is iden-tity as a human social production. The issue is this: What can we learn by an-swering the seminal question in sociological psychology terms and by defining identity as a totally social production?

As a totally social production, identity is a humanly constructed, defined, and sustained meaningful object. To be recognizably human, an organism must be interpreted as a meaningful identity; that is, as an object. An ''object'' is any reality toward which humans symbolically organize their responses and thus give it a meaning (Mead 1934). The object is socially meaningful to the extent that responses by others and by self fit together to reach the goals and embody the intentions of interacting individuals, as well as to represent the group's collective action. Yet human identity is a special meaningful object: It is both totally social and uniquely personal; it results from varying degrees of appropriation by self and/or bestowal by others. The dramatic quality of life flows in part from the endless negotiations of identities as self attempts to appropriate identities that others do not bestow, or others attempt to bestow identities that self does not appropriate.

How is it that identities are selves as ''meaningful objects'' that individuals can bestow or withhold, and appropriate or reject? The answer to this question derives from the particular reality of human identity. Identity is a definition that transforms a mere biological individual into a human person. It is a definition that emerges from and is sustained by the cultural meanings of social relationships activated in interaction. At the everyday empirical level, identity is available through language, the systems of codes by which humans define self and other. An empirically adequate treatment would have to include the myriad forms available in each historical period for defining selves. We intend ''definition'' in a broad sense to include nominal as well as qualifying terms. Indeed, the ''languages'' of gestures and appearances are also included.

Modern philosophy is conveniently dated from Descartes' double assertion, *Cogito ergo sum*. A sociological psychology of identity can be grounded in the recognition that ''I am'' implies the question, ''Who am I?'' An answer to the question ''Who am I?'' is an identity, a definition of an organism as a meaningful object of action within the category of human being.

''Who am I?'' is the seminal identity question that operationalizes the generic issue: How do we define a human being? Derived identity questions mirror its structure and point us toward the complex array of identities that constitutes a meaningful social world. A third party asks, ''Who is this individual?'' Indeed, the third party is led by natural English to bestow a gender identity by asking, ''Who is he?'' or ''Who is she?'' A second party, on the other hand, is forced by the English language to ask an individual in properly plural grammatical and, we shall argue, in properly plural sociological psychological form, but with an inaccurate biological reference – namely, ''Who *are* you?''

Addressing another person, a questioner faces a single biological individual, but must ask the seminal identity question in the plural – ''Who are you?'' Self can know the other only as an object, and since there are multiple definitions of any mere thing that make it into an object, the plural verb is socially appropriate. Analogously, the bestowal of gender identity and the singular verb in the third-party reference is culturally appropriate in a society based on the dichotomy of male–female gender identity, even though the sex of the identified person may be unknown or different from that which is addressed (cf. Stone 1970). In other words, answers to identity questions must be interpreted as meanings that define an individual as a social actor in the situation (Berger and Luckmann 1966: 159–65; Holland 1977).

Variants of the seminal question show additional masking of relevant socio-logical psychological meanings. Referring to a group of persons, we ask: "Who are they?" The form of the question masks the collective identity of the group *as such*. We are forced to identify the group as a plurality of individuals. We are forced to speak of it partitively rather than collectively. Similarly, if we ask about the identity of a group to which we belong, we are forced to ask: "Who are we?" Our thinking is channeled into a partitive view of the identity of a group as an aggregate of individuals, even though we are asking for the identity of the group as a group.

If we see a group of unusually tall males and ask "Who are they?" we expect the name of a basketball team, not a recitation of individuals' names. Similarly, if we are working to engender a collective identity in a group of young musicians and we were to intone rhetorically, "Who are we?" we expect "The Northside Junior Orchestra!" to be shouted back, not individual musicians' names. If, however, we wish to ask about the identity of a group as a group, we cannot ask, "Who is the team?" but must ask in an impersonal mode, "Which team is that?" Grammatical rules governing the structure of the seminal identity question do not allow us to ask about collective identity as individual and personal at the same time. We cannot ask, "Who is that orchestra?" although we seem close to being able to ask, "Who is that family?" indicating that family is the closest of any group to being coded as a personal reality.

To fill out the possibilities of the seminal question, and to break out of the cognitive limits of ordinary language, we need to violate grammar and unpack the meanings of human identity. First, as George H. Mead emphasized, self is experienced in two modes: spontaneously as a source and subject of action, an "I"; and reflexively as the object of action or the defined result of the responses of self and others, a "Me." Furthermore, we argue that the experience of "I" carries a concomitant sense of sameness and unity, a "substantival" sense of self (Weigert 1975). The experience of "Me," on the other hand, carries a sense of difference, a plural sense of self, since many others address us differently at different times.

The seminal identity question, "Who am I," must be paired with the grammatically barbarous but analytically liberating question, "Who are Me?" The "Me" is capitalized to show that it takes on the vocative function of direct address or reference, like a proper noun or the first-person nominative pronoun I. When the identity question is posed in the second-person situation, the correct form, "Who are you?" must be paired with the incorrect, ultimately unknowable, but more challenging form, "Who is you?" This second-person singular form is paired with the "Who am I?" that elicits the substantival sense of self, the incommunicable phenomenological sense of immediate subjectivity that is prepredicative and irreducible to social categories. It is therefore easily glossed in the language identity code of a pluralistic society. Yet the third-person form asks for a singular, gendered identity, "Who is he?" or "Who is she?" In the objective mode of the third-person reference, however, the more accurate social designation would be the grammatically incorrect "Who are he?" and "Who are she?" In everyday situations, we cannot easily ask for the plural identities of others that are not readily coded. They vary by situation and context, even though we assume a transsituationally constant person beyond the multiple identities (Guiot 1977).

In the plural forms of first- and third-person references, we are coded to think of the aggregation of persons partitively, as though we had to identify each individual to know who "they," the group, "are." In order to probe for a single collective identity, we would have to ask correctly, "Who is we?" and "Who is they?" Such a singular question about collective identity implicitly personifies the identity as well. Personification of a collectivity goes against the natural language assumption that only individuals are persons, whereas groups are thing-like objects. Yet organisms are not persons in the social ontological sense until they are properly and nominatively recognized as such. That is, identification of others, or personification, is a generic process in social life (Stone and Farberman 1970; Lichtenstein 1977; Robertson and Holzner 1979; Weigert 1983).

Analysis of the natural language of grammatically correct as well as incorrect answers to the identity question uncovers various meanings of identity. We find, paradoxically, that the answers are both uniquely individual and totally social. Whatever else identity is, it is always a socially intelligible definition of a uniquely individual reality, either personal in the case of singular human actors, or impersonal in the case of collective entities. Trying to define identity, we rediscover the perennial antinomies of the "one and the many," of public understanding and private experience, of personal appropriation and social imposition. The aim of this chapter is to begin formulating theoretical propositions and an order of analysis for grasping the experiences, definitions, and paradoxical processes of human identity.

One empirically available starting point is the sense of identity in a normally competent member of society who poses the seminal identity question for him or her self. In languages such as English that permit the form of the question "Who am I?" this self-addressed identity probe is an empirical and defined experience potentially available to all members of the language community. In the order of experience, self-awareness is primary. The order of analysis in our discussion, however, proceeds according to the socially real interactional arrangements available to normally competent adults. The primary and relatively unmediated datum of self-awareness that individuals take as the center of all that happens to them or that they do must be balanced against the mediated reality of the social order.

Within the broad limits of a sociological psychology, the opposite ontological pole from the unmediated immediacy of self-awareness is the opaquely mediated and derived reality of social structures that variously constrain and objectify personal experience, from unknown rules of language to public laws and bureaucratic organizations. The personal and social forms of identity are mutually constitutive, but in different modes. The constitution of identity parallels that of human social reality, in which self and society are mutually constitutive.

The order of analysis here does not recapitulate the order of personal development over the life course, nor the order of existential, situational awareness. Nor does the order of analysis reflect a sociologistic ontology that sees human reality determined completely by the forces and structures of society, language, or other a priori social realities. Personal developmental and existential issues, however, are illuminated by the analysis, since they are part of the total social fact of identity as a social production. Likewise, the a priori social structures are made intelligible as processes and objectivations constitutive of immediate experience defined as an identity to be validated in interaction.

Continuing the codification of the concept of identity, this chapter attempts to contribute to the development of what Sheldron Stryker (1977) called "identity theory" (cf. McCall and Simmons 1978; Robertson and Holzner 1979; Weigert 1983). We feel that the essential components for elaborating an identity theory are available, though we suffer no illusions about successfully completing the task here. We need to get on with the work, however.

A fundamental paradigm has emerged for conceptualizing identity: Identity is a socially constructed definition of an individual. As socially constructed, the definition of an individual makes use of culturally available meanings and distributes them according to rules of interaction and patterns of stratification. The meaning of an individual, then, derives from these socially constructed definitions – that is, his or her identities. A broad tradition exists for developing this paradigm from the work of "interpretive" sociologists such as symbolic interactionists, ethnomethodologists, and neo-phenomenologists. Finally, there is a vast and growing body of empirical work organized around the concept of identity, especially in the areas of deviance and substantive identities. Such work provides a basis for developing identity theory, although no synthesis of that large body of writings is attempted here.

This chapter summarizes representative writings around three key terms: meaning, self, and identity. Within these initial syntheses, an effort is made to formulate a set of propositions to codify what we can say about identity as a socially constructed reality. Note that we use the term "proposition" broadly, as the dictionary says: a proposal or offering; a project; an affirmation about a subject; a theorem to be demonstrated; or a subject to be discussed. We are not restricting the term to multivariate statements ready for testing. The general propositions set the stage for a definition of identity from a sociological psychology perspective. Finally, we touch all too briefly on selected themes relevant to identity in contemporary society.

Meaning

Central to a sociological psychology approach is the proposition that society is prior to the individual, as Goffman would say, "in every way" (1974: 13). We are concerned with the fundamental human issue of "ontogenesis," or the origin of individual persons as meaningful objects in sociohistorical contexts. We do not address the correlative and much more speculative issue of "phylogenesis," or the prehistorical origins of human species or of society. The genesis of individual beings as social objects is more or less empirically available to us; the origin of society or species-being is not.

A general agreement to focus on ontogenesis brings otherwise diverse theoretical orientations together for a brief but fundamentally important shared starting point. The formal, phenomenological type of analysis in the tradition of Simmel, the functional analysis of Parsons and contemporary followers, the conflict analysis of the power-oriented theorists, and the realist-oriented interactionists and social behaviorists in the tradition of George H. Mead all come together in their concern for what we may call the "societal imperative" – namely, society is prior to and shapes the individual. The societal imperative focuses attention on the processes of socialization that shape the raw material of the organism into a recognizably human person. We are never sure how much of personhood is due to societal forces, or to purely biogenetic or environmental factors, or to unique imaginative constructions of the individual in later phases of socialization. The societal imperative, however, teaches us to scrutinize symbolic action and the sociocultural meanings enacted in such action as the appropriate subject matter of a sociological psychology perspective on identity.

Symbolic action is always action within an already ongoing social life process

(Mead 1934). The social life process, furthermore, is one of interaction: mutually meaningful responses made by one actor to another such that each individual action is oriented in a larger and irreducible course of action which is intelligible to each actor and to a larger public. The generic assumptions that make the mutual orientation of interaction possible are constituted in the assumptive order of social structures and in the taken-for-granted world which appears real to each interactor individually and/or collectively. We see the most general and relevant assumptive structures to be those of power, which is widely studied though incompletely understood, and trust, which is relatively underdeveloped within the sociological enterprise (Luhmann 1979; Barber 1983; Lewis and Weigert 1985). Power and trust as assumptive structures provide deep interpretive procedures for making sense out of life. Cognitive forms and definitions of human action are seen as patterned and as sharing in some kind of larger meaning. Power and trust reduce the uncertainty generated by complexity, and underwrite the social and moral inferences by which persons link behavior and intention, as well as appearances and self (see Goffman 1959; Weigert 1981). The a priori reality of society grounds the first proposition of an incipient identity theory.

1. *Meanings are* realized – *that is, become known and behaviorally real* – *in mutually oriented responses according to the taken-for-granted* structures *of society, especially power and trust.*

From this general starting point, we move directly into the symbolic interaction tradition. In spite of common origin in the work of Mead, the symbolic interaction paradigm, in contrast to that of social behaviorism, finds its authoritative statements in the writings of Herbert Blumer (1969; see Lewis and Smith 1980). Blumer moves the central theoretical and empirical concerns from merely observable behavior to the symbolic transformation of that behavior through meanings, and the cognitive processes of interpretation through which the transformation takes place and is integrated into human interaction. The first step in the symbolic interaction enterprise is to transform all brute "things" of the mutely given environment into meaningful "objects" formed out of that environment by the selective and abstracting attention of human interactors. The meanings, in turn, are not taken from a Platonic heaven of timeless forms or a Kantian structure of a priori faculties. They emerge out of the give and take of the living interactional process itself. Each actor is an interactor mutually indicating meanings both to self and other.

Out of self and other indications, persons shape joint lines of action into emergent collective action and generate shared meanings that provide the so-called empirical structures of social life. The meanings, collective action, and structures that emerge are grasped by members of society through a process of interpretation according to the rules and organizing ideas which underlie that society. The opening sections of Blumer's (1969) seminal essay on methodology in symbolic interaction provide the foundation for the following propositions.

2. *Humans act toward things as objects on the basis of the meanings these objects (including humans) have for them.*
3. *Meanings emerge from symbolic interaction.*
4. *Meanings are grasped and applied through processes of learned interpretations.*

These three propositions generate a dialectical tension with proposition 1. They, and most of Blumer's theoretical writings, sound almost "creationist"; that is, persons seem to create objects, meanings, and courses of action out of whole cloth every time they interact. A Blumerian world is continuously created and re-created, like a spontaneous world of pure play. This creationist view of human social life flies in the face of the a priori reality of society stated in proposition 1. The resolution of the apparent contradiction parallels the perennial distinction mentioned above between "ontogenesis" and "phylogenesis," or the origin of the individual person and the origin of the species. Proposition 1 applies immediately to the empirical instances of each person's life. Society is prior in every way to what we may call "personogenesis," or the emergence of the biological individual as person through the process of socialization.

The message of proposition 1 is to affirm the ineluctible truth of a "social realist" position with reference to a central issue for understanding the human condition: What is the relationship between the individual and society? As such, the first proposition grounds identity theory in the original paradigm contained in the classical writings of the founders of sociology who, whatever their differences, in one way or another saw society as emergent and causative vis-à-vis the individual. Propositions 2–4, on the other hand, present the process of what we may call "societogenesis," or the continual constitution and reproduction of society through the actions, interpretations, and experiences of individuals. This represents the "social nominalist" position for understanding the relationship between the individual and society (see Lewis and Smith 1980). Theoretical reflection on identity must keep both the nominalist and realist positions in real tension, since both are needed for an adequate grasp of the total social fact of identity that incorporates individual existence as defined and meaningful persons (Berger and Luckmann 1966). Now we must address the process whereby merely individual behavior emerges as social action that continually reconstitutes the a priori reality of society.

Empirical study of humans living together easily finds patterns of mutually oriented responses. Empirical sociology documents endless examples of such action. These patterns are seen as "typical"; that is, as representative of the kind of action itself and as intelligible within the belief systems of those who enact the patterns and of those who observe or respond to these patterns through interpretations of them. The social life process, in other words, is selectively seen through the typifications persons have of objects in the meaningful environment, including other persons (Schutz 1962; Natanson 1974). The typifications are organized into the institutional order that makes up the society at this point in history.

The institutional order is grounded in the empirically available objective structures of meaning, such as language, procedures for interpreting actions and objects, taken-for-granted patterns of power and trust, rules for appropriate action, and rules governing how one is to feel and to interpret what one feels. The rather recent formulation of "feeling rules" enables us to understand how individuals come to believe that even their raw feelings constitute meaningful objective emotions through which they are related to the public order. Emotions, as defined feelings, enable individuals to feel at home in public domains varying from the most self-conscious and rationalized processes, such as bureaucracies, occupations, and educational experiences, to the most intimate and massively real existential encounters (see Hochschild 1975; Shott 1979; Gordon 1981; Weigert 1983, for statements toward a sociological psychology of emotions).

The mutual display and enactment of the institutional order provide the ontological foundation for what humans take to be existentially real and cognitively certain in their everyday lives. In contemporary society, this institutional order is further rationalized through its functional differentiation and formal organization into specialized units, such as businesses, schools, religions, governmental agencies, and so on. In summary, the systems of meaning *(Sinnzusammenhangen)* of contemporary society are objectivated in institutions that are functionally rational in terms of their operation and formally differentiated according to the demands of specialization. This characterization from classical sociological theory remains generally accurate for societal analysis and is safely applied to the interpretation of the relationships between the individual and society. Proposition 5 summarizes the way in which structures of meaning confront individuals in a complex contemporary society.

5. *Typical responses and meanings are formally and differentially objectivated in social institutions.*

Self

The institutional order of society reproduces itself, as it were, through the attitudes and actions of its members. Members of human society, by contrast with other animal societies, are conceptualized as "selves," and human society is organized by the symbolic constructions that simultaneously re-create society and socialize individuals. A human self is an organism that has the capacity for being simultaneously subject and object in a single act. Self is characterized by concomitant awareness both of acting and simultaneously of knowing that it is self who is acting (cf. Mead 1934; Weigert 1975). The full development of concomitant awareness apparently depends on the acquisition of symbolic competence. As humans come to use symbols, their consciousness acquires the capacity in critical situations to become *self* consciousness; that is, the individual reflexively becomes part of the symbolically transformed environment to which that individual responds (Ortega 1963; Weigert 1983a). At the same time, the social environment is constituted by the responses of other selves, each in turn with the capacity for reflexively activating his or her own self consciousness.

Individuals emerge as human selves through the responses of others. Although born to human parents, a totally and permanently isolated individual does not acquire the necessary means for existing humanly. These means are socially transmitted systems of public gestural and oral symbols. The process of becoming involves dimensions such as modeling, calculating rewards and punishments, and learning desirable social arrangements. A young girl, for example, acquires the self of an American female because she does what her mother does but not her father, or in her mother's style but not her father's, or what her mother asks her to do with an eye toward mother's rewards and punishments, or what the deep rules of gender display by other males and females render intelligible to her in everyday life. Similarly, an American learns to speak English because he or she imitates other English speakers, is rewarded or punished for correct or incorrect speech, and acquires the deep rules of grammar and language use before ever being taught what they are. Whatever the surface ''cause,'' individuals acquire, as part of their symbolic relationship to the social environment, internalized sets of rules, symbols, and interpretive procedures that enable them to live a life in terms of the meaning structures of that society, whether for good or ill. The organism becomes a human person in the very process of activating and acquiring the modes of its self as social. This process is summarized in proposition 6:

6. *Individuals become human as social selves by internalizing the institutionalized structures of meaning, such as language, interpretive procedures, action and feeling rules, social class perspectives, and so on.*

The institutionalization of human selfhood is never complete. There is always the dialectic between ''impulse'' and ''institution,'' or body and self, which marks the range of self orientation (Berger and Luckmann 1966:165–8; Turner 1976). In addition, as philosophical reflection from the sophists to the existentialists teaches us, the potentialities of the human imagination for thought and feeling, and the experience of concomitant awareness, defy reduction to, or total determination by, any social order. Finally, the structural pluralism of modern society ensures that a person relating to the relatively unintegrated institutional arrangements and plausibility structures experiences reverberations of that pluralism at the center of self (Berger et al. 1973; Bensman and Lilienfeld 1979). The experience of an impulse–institution or body–self dialectic, the potentialities of imagination, and t'~ pluralism of modern arrangements are within our intentional reach through   '~ and reflexivity (Husserl 1970).

The grounding detail (abstractions of human thought interact within   generate the uniquely human experience of s   ultiple self experience includes knowledge and   rent conceptualizations of human emotions fin   individual–society relationships. These relati   ules of feeling, vocabularies of emotion, an   that generate emotional involvements. Throu   al position and meaning are vivified within in   975; Kemper 1978; Shott 1979). The multipli   e variety of definitions of self as primordial e: ical construct.

From the social   ; viewed as emergent, as a "selfing" process   es and is shaped by the situational and cultu   nteraction takes place (Cottrell 1969; Lindes...   though other formulations of self have been offered, this view is co... the mainstream conceptualization of self found in current symbolic interaction literature. As a result, self is taken here to mean the evolving, self-aware production of a series of interactional relationships that lead to the development of the sense of individuality over the life course.

Identity is a "typified" or socially expressed dimension of self (Stone 1962). An individual has one self that becomes situationally typified through a variety of identities. Identities constitutes the "social self," or self in the context of social action. Goffman (1959) describes this as the "performed self" that is presented to others in the social actions of everyday life. Biddle (1979) refers to it as the "image," the set of identities and expectations that are structured by the social context or implied by the behaviors of others. Identity may be further subdivided into "personal" identity, based on characteristics presumably unique to the individual, such as style, organic markers, and so on; and "social" identity, based on broad social categories having general social acceptance (McCall and Simmons 1978). Putting these elements together, we see that identity is a system based on one's reflective view of self, perceptions of the expectations or response of others (reflected images), and subsequent reactions to shared reality or "validation" (Klapp 1969).

Validation is an integral part of the substantival self (Weigert 1975:51). Particular identities emerge from behaviors that are socially acted out. Validation occurs when another social actor recognizes and reacts to that identity. Thus, one successfully claims an identity only if the intended behavior becomes an "object" toward which others orient their behavior (Burke 1980; Stryker 1977). Identity is not a *spontaneous* product of the selfing process; it needs a mechanism through which it can be expressed. Social roles serve this function.

In his work on role theory, Biddle (1979:4) defines *roles* as "[patterned human] behaviors that are characteristic of persons within contexts and with various processes that presumably produce, explain, or are affected by those behaviors." Narrowing this view into our framework, role can be described as *expectations* that have been initiated by validated identities. These identities are manifested by performing various social roles and associated with certain appearances or attitudes (Weigert 1983). Once an identity is validated through role performance, the shift in temporal focus is to the past. For one to have an identity, there must be a vehicle (role) through which behaviors and expectations converge. Subsequently, the identity becomes validated and internalized, and one takes on this "new" identity to add to and synthesize with a growing repertoire of identities.

It should be noted that a central theme in the substantival self model is that a person is

[A] responsible agent, a member of society, a carrier and transmitter of culture, who yet is capable of setting himself apart from society and culture . . . , and who has a *continuous existence across situations and through time* within the boundaries of his or her own biography. (Weigert 1975:43, emphasis added)

This view implies that identities, as typifications of the self, display a degree of continuity in both expectations and behavioral expressions when roles are performed. However, as we will see later, this continuity may also be synthetically and artificially constructed in order to conceal an identity that is perceived as inconsistent with role expectations.

Roles do not exist in isolation, but serve as organizational links between individual and social structure (Stryker 1980). The structure is typically defined by bureaucratic organizations considered functional or necessary for the maintenance of social order, although nonbureaucratic institutions are also constituted by roles. Roles are associated with the stratification system, since they are linked to social positions within the power, class, and status structures of society. Status is attached to each position based on variations of valued resources, such as power and trust (Luhmann 1979; Lewis and Weigert 1985). As Biddle (1979:396, his emphasis) notes: "A position has higher *status* if its members have (or are presumed to have) more of some characteristic that is positively sanctioned, or if it regularly receives (or is presumed to receive) more of some positive sanction than some other position." There is a degree of interdependence between status and identity, since each has the potential of disdaining or enhancing the other to the extent that role performance is interpreted as an improvement on or inadequate to those expectations. Thus, individuals performing certain roles have the potential for raising the status of the position, just as one who becomes upwardly mobile and moves into a position accorded higher status has the opportunity to enhance perceptions about his or her identity.

The relationships among identities, roles, and organizations leads to the larger dialectic that occupies much of the sociological psychological literature, that between the individual and society (Mead 1934; Berger and Luckmann 1966; Blumer 1969; McCall and Simmons 1966; Schutz and Luckmann 1973). Just as roles link identity to the social structure, social structure through organizations reflects the needs and values of the larger society. This discussion is not intended to reflect either a psychological or social determinism in explaining the self–society dialectic. Regardless of whether one works downward from the macro-social level, or upward from the microself level, the relational layers remain the same. The scheme merely attempts to highlight the dimensions of the dialectic. The multiplicity of social self as experienced is summarized in proposition 7:

7. *Self is a multidimensional, reflexive, experiential process involving knowledge and emotion shaped by the individual's roles and social position.*

Identity

The multidimensional process of self is grasped by individuals and fashioned by society into meanings that are interpretable here and now. If it were not socially interpretable, personal experience would make no sense to us. Our indubitable center of personal experience would be nonsense, absurd. Our immediate self-hood would be a center of confusion and meaninglessness. The "facts" of identity contribute to our "sense" of personal identity, though they are not the same kind of reality (Harré 1983).

The self process must be "framed"; that is, organized into categories that enable individual experience to be symbolically transformed into social meanings. Such meanings make sense in terms of the transcendant sociocultural meaning system in which the individual lives (Goffman 1974). Following a Durkheimian lead, the raw "pre-meanings" of merely individual experience, even intimate experience of self, *must* be transformed into socially available meanings for personal experiece to be "real-ized"; that is, both made real and simultaneously made known as such. Otherwise, even our immediately available concomitant awareness of self in action or of organic rhythms would remain opaque, chaotic, and absurd to us. Human meaning, including self meaning, is a social fact, though it is never exhausted by social categories.

Individual experience of self, then, must be transformed into "objectificated" meanings. We use the term *objectification* to refer to the thinglike quality of self as an object among a world of objects. Objects are realities taken as originating from a source other than the self's own experiences and constituting a world that is out there independently of an individual's ability to wish it away or to transform it merely by thinking about it. As the phenomenological tradition teaches us, however, even the most thinglike of objects is a co-given reality both of an act of grasping, such as knowledge, desire, or feeling, and an object grasped, such as a rock, food, or lover.

What is unquestionably true of the human condition is that objects are constructed in accord with the grasping modalities of the human person. Objects are always in part, but in an essential part for human life, "in the making" – the root meaning of the Latin *facere* which, in combination with objects, gives us the word objecti-*fica*-tions. In everyday life, we are all engaged in a process of "making" the objects that structure our lives. And a central object is paradoxically also a subject; the most unique of objects is the human self. Self is an objectification. It is a reality in the making that is continually "thrown at or over" us, the meaning of the faded metaphors contained in the Latin roots of *jacere* (to throw) and *ob* (at, before, over, or against), as in words like "oblige," "obfuscate," "obstetric," or "obsolete." The total experience of self comes to each person as though from self *and* from other. Such is the inheritance of Western culture that splits everyday life and the objects which constitute that life into two independent sources that come together, however fleetingly, in each person's unified sense of self-awareness. As we insist, nevertheless, even the deepest and most intimate sense of self-awareness is itself an objectification, a socially constructed meaning.

Self-objectifications, furthermore, are experienced as under the control of self and of others. Self as a made object is experienced as subjective or objective, as defined and realized by self through "subjectivation," or defined and realized by others through "objectivation." The "other" may be another individual, group, or a generalized sociocultural organization of meanings (Mead 1934; Gerth and Mills 1964; Berger and Luckmann 1966; Klapp 1969). In all cases, however, self is an objectification, a constructed object of meaning. In order to understand the dynamics of identity, we must strip from the idea of subjective all connotations of biased, false, or mere opinion, and from the idea of objective all connotations of unbiased, true, and evidential. Both processes, subjectivation and objectivation, generate a version of self as a real object within available sociocultural systems of meanings.

An adequate identity theory must keep both processes in view by allowing conceptual development and methodological procedures for each. In this way, we strive to grasp the essential sociological dynamic of human life as a process of fitting the subjectivation and objectivation of self as social object into an integrated and continuous totality experienced as *my* real self in an authentic and plausible life (Erikson 1978). The normally indubitable experience of self as *my* real self is a given fact, and a most intimate one at that. For this reason, it is not a fact originating from a mysterious source beyond the pale of sociological understanding. Indeed, the verisimilitude and indubitability of the experience of identity with self is itself a social fact. "Self identity" is a meaningful redundancy only because the possibilities of self alienation loom large. Trying to understand the genesis and sustenance of self identity enables us to probe the point of conjunction between social and personal reality, a Cartesian point of unity between society and self, as it were.

Identity theory forces us to go beyond even the facilely accepted Cartesian truth for grounding all interrogation of reality. *Cogito ergo sum* – "I think, therefore I am" – does not guarantee that "I am who I think I am." Yet in the act of thinking about self, everyone must think of self as an identified somebody. There simply is no empirically disembodied thinker floating beyond the reach of sociocultural meanings. Every thinker must go a step further and reenter the real world; he or she must identify self as a historically and circumstantially real person (Ortega 1961). At the moment of self-identification, the entire problematic of self-objectification must be addressed, and the necessity for a sociological psychology of identity becomes apparent. We are forced by the paradoxical necessity of historicity to give an essential but contingent answer to the question of self-identity. We must answer; it is essential. But every answer is a conventional construction; it is a historical contingency. As José Ortega y Gasset insisted so petulantly, the answer can come only within the confines of historical reason true to the paradigm, "I am myself plus my circumstance." The human condition is grounded on a paradox of identity: The best answer anyone can give to the necessary modern question about self is a contingent and historically limited reply. It is a typification of self until further notice. Part of the thesis of this book is that such a historical realization is a unique, emergent, and perhaps definitive feature of modern life.

The dialectic of personal and public objectifications of self provide the grounding for typologies of personality that analysts have constructed, such as Merton's anomie paradigm relating character to sociocultural means–ends, or Riesman's inner- versus other-directed character. Objectifications of self occur at different levels of social reality. A reasonable paradigm includes five levels based on the relationship between self and other: ego, individual, group, organizational, and societal (see Goffman 1963; Stone and Farberman 1970; Mol 1976). Societal objectifications are those empirically available to normal members of society in the particular historical period. They are the most general and apparent objectifications, such as gender, age, health, and in American society, ethnicity/race. Organizational objectifications are those that derive from the more formal institutions structuring the society. In modern times, the organizing principle is generally a bureaucratic one; organizational objectifications are likely to be titles associated with positions in a bureaucracy.

Group objectifications are realized within the groups that work as reference realities defining the individual through associational ties (Schmitt 1972). Such reference groups are increasingly diverse as modern society becomes more complex and its members more mobile, either as a result of social exigency or their own choice. At the individual level of objectification, the individual is symbolized through such media as personal names, labels with individuating content, and paradoxically in a bureaucratic society, through that general symbol system that simultaneously objectifies individual realities: numbers. The rationalization of modern society is reflected through the use of numbers for objectifying everything from streets and houses to social security, taxes, intelligence, and even the person. The fifth objectification of self is that which we call ''ego,'' following Goffman (1963), but not a strict psychoanalytic or psychiatric use. Self as ego refers to objectifications as felt, internalized, and appropriated, or resisted by the individual, or attributed by others as presumably felt by self. Ego brings us as close to the premeaningful reality of the stream of consciousness, self experience, and deep interpretive procedures as we can get with our present paradigm.

Across the five levels of social psychological reality, the dialectic between personal or subjective and public or objective dimensions holds. Typically, we expect that public objectivation increases as we move across the levels of ego, individual, group, organizational, and societal reality, whereas the subjective sense of personal identity decreases. Conversely, the sense of personal identity typically increases as we move in the opposite direction from the level of societal reality to that of ego. At neither extreme, however, do we lose either sense of identity, at least not typically nor completely, although merger with a public identity or submersion into an ego-identity is possible. Such extremes would render the person unfit for the range of everyday interaction.

In the routine activities of everyday life, the objectifications of self normally ''fit'' the level of reality in which we are acting. Captains of jumbo jets cannot typically daydream about stock market coups as they are in the midst of landing in a snowstorm. Nor do lovers worthy of the name analyze their social status as they reach for each other. The fit of self and objectification, however, is not so orderly by natural necessity, but as an ultimately precarious achievement of individuals. Telling and extreme character types can be generated by changing the fit between self and objectification. Severe autism in a child like Joey can lead him to think of himself as a real machine (Bettelheim 1967). Joey illustrates the rare instance of extreme objectivation at the level of ego. On the other hand, an individual caught up in a public identity may merge his or her consciousness into that symbolic role and become a totally public person (Turner 1978). The original Lone Ranger went to court to argue his self-defined and sole right to wear the Lone Ranger mask in public.

The issue at hand is this: How closely do different types of objectifications dominate an individual's sense of the experience of self that is taken to be real? To what degree does the individual merge existentially with one or the other type of self experience that is socioculturally available? As Erikson wondered in his early work: How can a young Sioux male achieve a stable sense of self now that the dominant identity of warrior is no longer available? In a word, how do certain sets of symbols representing different levels of social reality come to function as objectifications of self and to be internalized as existentially real identities? These issues are reflected in proposition 8:

8. *Dimensions of self are transformed into meaningful objects as subjective and objective identities at the analytic levels of ego, individual, group, organization, and society.*

A characteristic feature of complex society, then, is that many and changing definitions of self are available as identities. One or another identity may be presented by self or imposed by others as each negotiates for control of the situation. Individuals are faced with the task of continually managing multiple identities within and across situations. The management of multiple identities is both a structural consequence of the organization of society and a dramaturgical task for attaining the business at hand (Goffman 1959; Blumer 1969; Stryker 1980; Weigert 1983).

The institutional order of society includes an ordering of identities into salience hierarchies that reflect the distribution of trust and power. Priests are likely to be trusted more than politicians, but politicians typically have more power in American society. A priest-politician, therefore, is likely to have difficulty arranging multiple identities into a hierarchy that fits with the salience hierarchy built into the institutional order of society and that can secure the task at hand. The problem is especially acute if the priest is a woman or if the pope prohibits priests from the political identity. Church–state relations parallel the social psychological relations of priest or preacher and politician from contexts as different as the United States, Ireland, and revolutionary societies in Latin America or the Near East.

Even if the a priori structure of multiple identities is stably arranged, the identities must still be enacted effectively in various situations. This is the quintessential dramaturgical task. In routine situations, the salience hierarchy of identities relevant to the task at hand is enacted perhaps without coming into explicit awareness. In problematic situations, however, the performer confronts a task as precarious and delicate as the relevant identity is crucial and difficult (see Hewitt 1979:124–32; Burke 1980). Solutions to the problem of which identity to enact here and now are derived from the a priori institutional order that defines the demand characteristics in the situation and from the individual's felt probabilities of successfully enacting an identity and attaining the task at hand. The management of multiple identities finally depends on the dramaturgical skills of the individuals engaged in the interaction. This point is made in proposition 9, which recognizes that multiple identities are typically organized into salience hierarchies.

9. *Multiple identities are enacted according to salience hierarchies based on the a priori institutional order, the felt probabilities of success, and the dramaturgical skills of the performers in the situation.*

The enactment of identities involves the presentation of select dimensions of self. Common sense may suppose that presenting self is totally under a performer's control. Social psychology, however, shows that dimensions of self may be imposed by others, result from team performance, or issue from unintended appearances.

Garfinkel (1956) outlines an interaction process in which a negative identity is forcefully imposed on an unwilling recipient. A young woman claiming innocence is publicly proclaimed guilty of murder at a criminal trial in a court of law and forcefully jailed for life; an adult man is publicly court-martialed, stripped of all privileges, and dismissed from the army on charges of collaborating with the Vietcong against his own country; a young child is publicly denounced for cheating on an English test, accused of violating the standards of the school, and given an F grade in front of his classmates – each of these scenes represents what Garfinkel calls a "degradation ceremony."

A degradation ceremony is "any communicative work between persons, whereby the public identity of an actor is transformed into something looked on as lower in the local scheme of social types . . ." (Garfinkel 1956: 420). If we assume that no normal citizen desires a negative or "lower" identity in the moral ranking, then a degradation ceremony involves the coercive imposition of a demeaning identity on an unwilling recipient. The ceremonial order of human life includes the offering of deference, or appreciation for a person, and the enactment of demeanor, or the expression of the unique valued qualities of a person (Goffman 1967). In a degradation ceremony, the value of a person is negated: A person, like bad money, is depreciated; and he or she is forced to act in a demeaning way, like sitting in a corner, wearing a dunce cap, kneeling obeisantly, or kissing a superior's foot.

Degradation ceremonies are not always successful, however. Persons whose identities are being devalued may actually seek to devalue them or, paradoxically, succeed in devaluing the identities of those presiding over the ceremony. In these cases, the ceremony is used by the "victims" to attack the reigning institutional order. By turning the tables, the victims of the ceremony degrade the identities of those presiding over it. In the late 1960s, for example, a group of radical "revolutionaries" were put on trial in Chicago for conspiracy against the government of the United States. Rather than accept the court's attempt to define them as morally inferior persons, the revolutionaries attacked the court as a repressive institution and Judge Hoffman as a Hitler character demonstrating the moral sickness of American society. In response, Judge Hoffman attacked the defendants and acted outside the usual rules of judicial decorum (Antonio 1972). The Chicago "trial" became an unsuccessful degradation ceremony in which the defendants' identities were not devalued in their eyes or in the judgment of their reference groups. Rather, the defendants affirmed their revolutionary message by eliciting uncourtly behavior by the judge, who thereby devalued his identity and the American judicial process in the eyes of critical Americans.

Human life may be interpreted as a dance of deference and demeanor, as a series of simple ceremonies in which we bestow, validate, or threaten our own and others' valued sense of self announced through publicly presented identities. Indeed, we argue that the ceremonial order of society supports whatever solidity we give to our precarious sense of self identity or to that awareness which grounds each person's momentarily unquestioned but always questionable conviction that he or she is really the person he or she thinks is real here and now. Through the ceremonial order, we perform and make experientially available a historical sense of self that is missing from the overly abstract Cartesian experience of a primordial self as merely existing. Realized identities are rooted in the processes of ceremonial communication.

The range of dramaturgical control and the necessity of appearing to self and others brings us to the next issue: the communication of identity. Communication as a social process and interactional demand is so far-ranging that its adequate understanding involves disciplines from animal ethology to ahistorical semiotics, and from data as diverse as naturalistic studies of insects to artificially produced computer languages. The link between communication and identity is yet to be completely forged, if it ever can be. For present purposes, we can do not more than touch upon salient dimensions relevant to sociological psychology.

Communication of identity introduces the apparently and literally superficial reality of human appearances. The reality of appearances, in turn, raises the issue of the relationship between appearances and "who is really there." Analysts have noted the importance of appearances in relation to the reality of self and the attendant problems of misrepresentation versus true knowledge of self (Goffman 1959; Stone 1962; Husserl 1970; Ichheiser 1970). From the point of view of the public other, the appearances of self are the underlying warrant and guarantee for making an identification of that self.

Paradoxically, of course, the very necessity of interpreting appearances to identify a person makes it possible to hide the "true" relationship between appearances and self and to engage in misrepresentation, deception, lies, and feigning of all sorts. The link between appearances and the self is itself never visible; it is an inferred link. The inferential reality of that link offers the opportunity for a person who does not wish to be recognized to break the typically assumed true link between appearances and self. On the other hand, those who do not wish to believe in the truth of the link, and who do not wish to affirm that a person is who he or she appears to be and claims to be, can insist on doubting that link no matter how much self begs to be accepted for the person he or she indeed truly is. This experience is known to anyone who has tried in vain to cash a check knowing that there is enough money in the account; or tried in vain to enter a guarded building or restricted party knowing that he or she qualifies for entrance even without the ID card left at home; or tried in vain to convince a doctor that he or she is really sick even though there are no symptoms that fit an illness profile. Furthermore, appearances that are falsely linked to self can be fateful. Persons have been falsely accused, convicted, and executed on the basis of self linked to appearances as circumstantial evidence and through the supposedly accurate testimony of even eyewitnesses. Through it all, the wrongly accused person knows that she or he is innocent, but cannot disprove the incriminating appearances.

Successfully representing self in order to elicit a derived identification from another involves the entire individual, from external appearances to intention and desire (Goffman 1959; Weigert 1983). Only those aspects of self that are publicly validated, however, become really fateful, because only they enter the interactional reality out of which identities are constructed. Wishful thinking bears no offspring, but our actions and appearances become our fate. An individual may manipulate a particular situation through a partial presentation or masking of self with a reasonable chance of success even in the misrepresentation itself. On the other hand, an entire life of masking a hidden identity that contradicts a presented one, such as the life of a secret adulterer or double spy, demands total control over relevant appearances. A single slip in identity maintenance with the wrong audience threatens to discredit the doctored appearances and to lay bare the hidden identity. The difficulty with living a lie is that no one can be sure of controlling every bit of identifying appearances at every moment. A true identity requires typical preparation; it is false identities that demand a person's totally artful attention.

To be an identified self is to be a "displayed" self. *Display* means to "fold apart" or "unfold" into meaningful patterns of interaction and symbolic presentation that communicate self. The term is borrowed from ethologists, and its use for the communication of human identity is apt. The kind of communication involved in presenting self for identification is indeed display; it is behavior rendered meaningful as interaction; it is interaction interpreted as symbolic manifestations of self. Humans must appear to one another; they must act toward each other; and they normally engage in a generalized symbolic medium of mutual presentation constituted by language and gesture. Each of these modes of presentation of self follows its own intrinsic logic of display. Each is the object of a number of separate disciplines, and each discipline defines separate objects found nested in its methodological and theoretical paradigms from fashion to metalinguistics.

In addition to the literal content of the message communicated through each of these modalities, identity is simultaneously and necessarily communicated as well. Every moment of our lives can be interpreted as an identity display and probed for the meaning it contains relevant for knowing the identities of the displayer. This necessity to appear and to communicate identity along with every message is contained in proposition 10:

10. *Multiple identities are communicated through displays of appearances, behavior, and language.*

Displays do not merely communicate identity to others, however. They also communicate identity to self, both through the inner "propriosensation" of kinesthetic and self imagery available to the performer, and through the interactional interpretation made of the display in subsequent responses by others. Classical symbolic interaction theory emphasizes the interactive process in the "looking-glass self," or mirror theory of identity. The mirror theory argues that we are what others' reflections make us. In addition, however, we are also what we sense ourselves to be in our inner conversation within the private forum of self-consciousness and concomitant self-awareness. Displays, then, construct identities in the minds, feelings, and responses of others, and simultaneously in the mind, feelings, and actions of self. Identity is produced as a social object by the two processes of subjectivation and objectivation. We construct ourselves as we display ourselves to others. We become what we show ourselves to be to others and self (see Gecas 1982).

The idea of identity construction through the responses of self and others to our displays of self follows immediately from a Meadian triadic approach to meaning and from conceptualizing identity as a totally social meaning. Displays, however, are not solely free play or creative innovation. Rather, the a priori institutional order and present situational context shape a person's "commitment structure." A person displays an identity because she or he is committed to that identity by self and for others. Commitment refers to a structure of meanings constituting our self experience, both that which we hold in awareness and that which may be temporarily out of awareness. Identities are part of this structure of meanings. The ordering of identities in terms of the degree and kind of commitment each interactor has to them constitutes the *identity commitment structure,* which is given a priori in the situation. The structure both derives from the institutional order or society and is activated situationally in accord with the demands facing the person about to perform and the audience about to witness the performance (Becker 1960; Kanter 1972; Turner 1978; Stryker 1980).

Cutting across the institutional order and articulating with the immediate situation is the sociotemporally generated reality of a person's stage in the life course (see Erikson 1978). Every known society apparently has definitions of identities based on stages in the life course from infancy to what we may call anciency. These definitions also are part of the a priori institutional order and constitute a set of objective identities that is imposed on the life course and transforms it into a socially interpretable biography. As persons are continually socialized into each period of their lives, these objective identities are more or less appropriated by self and become part of their subjective identities. Identity socialization is a dynamic social process, and not a mere mechanical realignment. The interpretive procedures of individuals, the interactional dynamics of social life, and the institutional logics of society together shape the appropriation and imposition of identities to the contingencies of history and the biographical situation of the individual (see Sheehy 1976; Gubrium and Buckholdt 1977; Levinson 1978; Rubin 1981). The intersection of a priori institutional structures and the individual's life course generates human biography – that is, a meaningfully constructed story of a person's life (see Mills 1959; Berger 1963; Goffman 1963; Daily 1971). The intersection of society and life course is reflected in the structure of identity commitments experienced within a person's biography. This intersection is indicated in proposition 11:

11. *Commitment to identities results both voluntarily and involuntarily from an individual's biography, which incorporates both position in the social structure and stage in the life course.*

Persons committed to one or another identity must still meet the structural demands of fashioning action in accordance with the logic and assumptions of the situation to achieve the significance they seek. The imperative to act significantly links the inner experience of each participant into a system of meanings realized in interaction. This link is conceptualized by seeing persons as performers of roles; that is, shared expectations mobilized by validated and committed identities in the social situation (see Stone and Farberman 1970; McCall and Simmons 1978; Biddle 1979; Turner 1978; Weigert 1983; Zurcher 1983).

Roles link persons and social structure. Seen from the side of a priori structure, roles refer to sets of demands, rights, and obligations associated with positions in social organizations. Seen from the side of interactional situations, roles refer to actors' expectations present in and shaping their attitudes toward the social act. Structural or institutional demands are realized more or less consistently in the living expectations and interactions of persons actually present to the encounter (Goffman 1961a; Turner 1962; Lindesmith et al. 1977). Roles may be the rigid rules of asylums or the intimate patterns of love affairs. Persons not only enact a priori roles, they "make" existential roles. And in so doing, they simultaneously make identities for themselves and each other. Roles are performed in accord with the identities that are realized or projected here and now.

The selection of identities relevant to the situation was addressed above in the discussion of multiple identities. Now we are faced with the issue of choosing the proper course of action, a course of action that is always to some degree meaningful as a result of its "typicality" and predictability (Schutz 1962). Social action is oriented in its course to the probable responses of others. After the preliminary and largely assumptive, or taken-for-granted and unrecognized, interactional work of accepting identities and choosing potential roles, individuals must align their systems of relevance with those structured into the situation and/or carried by others who are present. As Schutz develops the idea of relevance systems, individuals construct social action by recognizing what is the topic governing action; what interpretive frame is likely to apply to the topic; and which motivational scheme is appropriate to the action once it is properly recognized and interpreted (Schutz 1970; Weigert 1975a; cf. Goffman 1974). In the situation, relevance systems are linked to the structure of identities, expectations, and commitments that are at stake and that each person is likely to display. Action is likely to be in accord with the identities to which we are committed (see Stryker and Serpe 1982). This leads us to proposition 12:

12. *Selves are committed to roles that are relevant to their identities.*

Toward a definition of identity

Up to this point, we have operated with a commonsense notion of identity. Identities are labels, names, and categories through which persons address each other and themselves. They are patterned ways of speaking, thinking, feeling, and performing that have as their object the interpersonal relations that constitute the identity (Scheff 1970). Identities originate in socially constructed, objectivated, and institutionalized meanings. They work as commitments and are negotiated and displayed by persons who experience them as both subjective and objective realities. Their function is to allow the scene to come off by preventing or answering challenges and questions directed at individuals. The questions are both self-originated and other-originated; they are both singular and plural, subjective and objective; they sometimes make sense socially, grammatically, and existentially; and sometimes they do not.

Identities are answers to questions such as these: What am I? Who are you? Who are me? Who are I? The grammatical barbarities are necessary to hint at the range of meanings that self, others, and society construct and impose on persons. Nor do all the identities have to make sense or be integrated into a neat totality, as though a modern person were a walking equilibrium or homeostatic system. The tragic, comic, mundane, and transcendent meanings of biography are not adequately captured in the neat, grammatical, and consistent rationality of conventional social science puppets. The boundaries of neat rationality need to be broken on occasion to remind us that human existence is a "vital rationality" driven by the demands of life, and not by those of science (Ortega 1961; Schutz 1962; Garfinkel 1967).

A working definition of identity needs to reflect the dialectical pluralism and tensions of modern life while holding on to the unique personal dimensions of biography. It must recognize the concreteness of present situations and the apriority of the institutional context. It builds on the assumption that self is active, and it notes that self must be somehow typical to be intelligible. Typicalness derives from social organization and realized social relationships. These considerations suggest the following definition (see Stone and Farberman 1970):

Identity *is a typified self at a stage in the life course situated in a context of organized social relationships.*

This definition combines the abstract features of typicalness, apriority, organization, sociality, relatedness, and development. Guided by these abstract features, humans "fill in" the sentient details and experiential immediacy of the social life process to construct living persons out of the doll-like abstractions. This last sentence, of course, is an analytical description. Individuals in real life are not conscious of any such filling in; vital reason operates in the mundane taken-for-granted world of the natural attitude, which works without self-conscious attention. Our statement is a rational reconstruction that sees the abstractions and thinks of individuals filling in the sentient and experiential reality. The justification for such rational reconstruction, apart from the quest for conceptual clarity, is to uncover crucial identity issues in people's lives. Analytical reconstruction should enable us to address those issues more adequately. The next section hints at the potential payoff from these formulations.

Issues concerning identity

The utility of the propositions and the definition of identity is gauged by the fruitfulness of the issues it brings into view and of the interpretations it generates. We would like to touch briefly and theoretically on five issues that seem relevant to our present historical juncture. The issues assume clear recognition of the principle that only those kinds of identities can be realized which are socially available to an individual during his or her lifetime. Who we can be is limited by the times in which we live.

The crisis of modernity brings to the fore the underlying dialectics of subjective and objective features of identity. From the perspective of philosophical anthropology, this dialectic is a human necessity. Only in societies organized and interpreted pluralistically, however, does the anthropological necessity become a cultural and personal issue as well. The pluralistic organization of society is reflected in the multiplicity of identities bestowed on and experienced by modern individuals. Every person is faced with the daily task of organizing his or her multiple identities successfully. In addition, the extent of change and contradiction accompanying the multiplicity of identities generates concern for the continuity of identity. This concern is typically but inadequately defined in psychological terms as a personal problem, thus masking the underlying historical and social dynamics (Wexler 1983). Finally, these identity issues are experienced within the emotional life of individuals. A fundamental sense of "dis-ease" with self and lack of coherent public meaning for basic feelings marks modern consciousness as narcissistic, bored, apocalyptic, or materialistic. Material gadgets, self-scrutiny, quick fixes, or distracting thrills are sought as answers to fundamental identity issues. Let us briefly address these issues.

The dialectic of subjective and objective identity

At the base of the identity problematic lies the subject-object dialectic that has so occupied Western thinkers since Hegel's time. This dialectic is an anthropological necessity; it is a generic feature of human life (Ortega 1961; Berger and

Luckmann 1966). In more homogeneous traditional societies, we assume that the dialectic of subjective and objective moments in human identity is part of the public domain, part of the collective rituals and beliefs. As a totally public reality, the dialectic does not emerge as a separate process in the existential condition or personal experience of individual consciousness. Nevertheless, as long as humans possess the capacity for reflexivity, the dialectic is at work, quietly and unattended, in the natural attitude dominating awareness in everyday life.

In modern society, however, the dialectic of subjective and objective identity has come into awareness with a vengeance and as a central, perhaps *the* central, issue facing each person in search of a meaningful life. Identity has become a private reality developing within the personal responsibility of each individual, and generating the profound personal emotions of self-esteem or self-hate. Modern persons find themselves "between public and private" with no undoubted, satisfying public definition of self, nor secure and convincing private sense of self-identity (Berger 1967; Klapp 1969; Bensman and Lilienfeld 1979). The dialectic of subjective and objective identities, in other words, has taken incarnate shape in modern society (see Holland 1977).

Without stretching the idea of the dialectic beyond recognition, we discern its working in the process by which an immediately experienced sense of individual self is realized in the context of an a priori institutional order. The process of realization is a mode of praxis, an identity praxis of dramatic interaction producing a plausible identity for self and others. This vital dialectical process stretches across time as it both issues from and results in more or less plausible identities. These identities struggle to grasp the immediate realism of personal experience and the mediated reality of others' responses in a single interpretive act. The act of interpretation within the natural attitude produces a single social act out of the myriad behavioral and sentient individual realities. That social act is experienced as validating or threatening each interactor's presented identity and, by implication, his or her sense of being an integrated person. Action sustains our sense of identity.

The "humanness" of a person's life emerges from delicate interpersonal work. It is not a genetically programmed biological unfolding, like the petals of a flower. Humanness is a quality of our peculiar form of animal life. As such, humanness is an object that emerges from the dialectic of subjectivation and objectivation by which human animals in fact produce their identities. We would offer a new definition of human nature as *animal identicatum*. The dialectic offers firm grounding for a dramaturgical perspective in sociological psychology without resort to alienated cynicism, ideological fanaticism, or the narcissistic necessity of being self-consciously "on" as we live our everyday lives (Messinger et al. 1962). Such criticisms of dramaturgy and Goffman's work miss the metaphysical nature of the dialectical relationship between the moments of subjectivation and objectivation in the social life process through which everyone's self-identity is realized (see Wilshire 1982: 274–81).

The dialectic grounds the essential tragic and comic perspectives on human life. A theoretical point of view that loses either moment of the dialectic flattens human life into a reduced condition of mechanical idealism or abstracted empiricism. In such reduced conceptual states, human life offers no justification for a tragic or comic interpretation. Yet these interpretations are perennial stuff for probing the depths of what it really means to be human. A touchstone for the adequacy of a theoretical paradigm of human action is whether or not it makes the tragedy and comedy of life more intelligible. Ultimately, the "meaning of life" develops into an interrogation of the fit between subjectivated identities and objectivated identities and the vital tensions between them. A particularly modern type of "problem in living" (Szasz 1967) arises from the poor fit between the two kinds of identity. This "mis-fit" is a characteristic of mental illness, with its anxiety, depression, boredom, and general symbolic disarray (Laing 1972).

Human life, as Ortega y Gasset insisted, is a form of vital reason: reason in the service of authentic human life, guided by the meaningful demands of our sociohistorical situation. All of culture is an interpretation of a human life. The dialectic of subjective and objective identity leads us into the question of historically available types of identity.

The sociohistorical availability of identities

Individuals can be personified only in terms of the identities that are real at the time. Dreamers think of themselves in any number of identities from Roman senators, to medieval knights, to contemporary revolutionaries. Once dreamers awaken, however, they can realistically identify themselves only with those identities that are empirically available in the historical period and social position in which they are living. Whether they can be a "hero, artist, sage, or saint" depends on the availability of these identities (see Coan 1977).

In our lifetime, a number of identities became available for the first time. In the 1930s and 1940s, a space traveler was a fantasy identity like Buck Rogers or Flash Gordon. By the 1970s, however, it became a real identity in the persons of Soviet cosmonauts or American astronauts. What was fantasy in an earlier period became a socially available identity in a later one. Another example is provided by medical technology that brought the identity of a "postoperative transsexual" into the institutional order of contemporary society (see Kessler and McKenna 1978). Persons who beocme postoperative transsexuals are pioneering a new identity.

Worldwide ideologies competing for dominance carry within themselves different types of identities in other areas as well. Analysis of a contemporary capitalistic society such as the United States sees a transition from an inner-directed traditional person to an other-directed modern person and on to a narcissistic, inward-turning contemporary person in search of meaning within the world view of bourgeois individualism (see Riesman et al. 1950; Lasch 1979). American culture is pervaded by a nominalist psychologistic bias lending plausibility to a natural attitude that sees atomistic individuals responsible for their fate, happiness, and especially success or failure. Totalitarian states, on the other hand, generate their own identities, such as loyal party *appartchik,* teenage martyr, fanatic revolutionary, or so-called student in search of immortality through destruction of traditional social forms, as in China of the 1960s, or through a vanguard of reactionary revolution, as in Iran of the 1970s.

Extending the concept of identity to representative social types, we see the emergence of central identities in rapidly evolving Third and Fourth World countries. The rush to religion in the service of autochthonous nationalism characterizes some societies seeking an alternative to both capitalist and Communist identities. The religiopolitical identity types of *mullah* or *ayatollah,* for example, become central representative identities wielding power in reactionary Islamic theocracies. At the same time, typical Western bourgeois identities, especially for women, are opposed, thus creating imposing difficulties for those seeking such identities.

In general, authority structures built into different institutional orders generate sets of empirically available identities with which members of these societies can realize the meaning of their lives (see Robertson and Holzner 1979). Through all the change and complexity, modern individuals struggle to control their lives by organizing the mix of personal identities into a meaningful arrangement of biographical importance and situational flexibility within an increasingly rational and abstract social context (Zijderveld 1971).

The organization of multiple identities

The complexity, anonymity, and mobility of modern society are reflected in the identity structures of its members. Individuals have multiple identities. These identities must be organized – that is, functional – within the a priori institutional order; arranged in a hierarchy of importance to the self; fitted to the hierarchy of importance expected by others; and flexible enough to be adapted to situational demands.

In everyday life, persons tend to assume a simplified model of self presenting a single identity in the situation. Now, however, we must think in terms of a more complex and realistic model of presenting an organization of multiple identities that is always implied by the presentation of that single identity. If a man presents the identity of "loving husband" to his wife, others simply assume that the rest of his identities are meaningful organized around that identity, and that his life makes sense by interpreting his identities as so organized. If, however, his secretary knows that, without his wife's knowledge or acquiescence, he is having an affair with the lady who lives down the block, then a different interpretation of the organization of his multiple identities must be made to get an accurate picture of him as a complete person. The identity of "unfaithful husband" in the context of a duplicitous marriage leads an observer to interpret the presented identity, loving husband, in such a way as to contradict the normal interpretation made by others, including the wronged and uninformed wife. Those who know about his hidden identity interpret the loving husband identity as a front, while those who do not know of the hidden identity see him as loving, as he appears to be.

The task of organizing multiple identities comes to the fore in times of social change and at critical decisions within the life course. As women begin to pursue occupational careers and work outside the home, they and their families are faced with the task of rearranging the multiple identities of redundantly labeled "working women." In some and perhaps critical situations, the identity of wife needs to be subordinated to that of worker or professional. Reordering women's identities creates problems within patriarchal marriages. The traditional "total woman" who is wife-mother-homemaker without extradomestic employment does not have this problem of organizing her identities. A young adult facing a major career decision of whether to go to college or to apprentice as a bricklayer must struggle with the organization of his or her identities and try to discern which makes sense in terms of those more or less clear aspirations motivating him or her right now. In modern society, even an individual's identities must be rationalized and planned. Such planning is a psychological characteristic of modern social organization (Berger et al. 1973).

Individuals offer for validation a master identity that represents an implied organization of all other identities. The issue of multiple identities does not consciously surface in routine situations in which each participant's presented identity and implied organization of other identities is simply taken for granted. In problematic situations, however, persons experience doubt about each other and eventually about themselves. No one is sure who to be or why. Participants have doubts about which identity to present and how to present it, or about whether the presented identity is validated and to what extent (Hewitt 1979). Too much identity doubt makes planning difficult and leads to deeper doubt about self.

As individuals enter a situation and seek to act effectively, therefore, they must present an organization of multiple identities arranged into hierarchies of salience appropriate to the kind of person they wish to be, the course of action they want to pursue, and the shared meaning they seek to construct (Foote 1951; Goffman 1959; Burke 1980; Stryker 1980). If it is a problematic situation, the dramaturgical imperative of effective stagecraft becomes the explicit focus of attention. The problematic dramaturgical task focuses the work of the interactors. They act to construct a working consensus that will enable each of them to be the kind of person they want to be without threatening each other's presented identity or the implied organization of their multiple identities. Routine, non-problematic situations hide the dramaturgical work as identities are presented, negotiated, validated, and exchanged without perceived threat and with a sense of existential ease. Situational "dis-ease," or being ill at ease, however, indicates identity problems and alienation from the interaction, from those present, and from self. Left unresolved, such dis-ease may generate mental "illness," or problems in living.

Ease of interaction displays the normality of what is happening. Problematic situations are characterized by a sense of being personally "on stage." When an individual feels "on," the taken-for-granted and undoubted self-consciousness of one's presented identity is lost, and a dramaturgical consciousness emerges (Messinger et al. 1962). Anyone faced with a problematic situation is in a difficult spot and is likely to feel "on." Such a live performer must control the inner flow of feelings and consciousness, including that which constitutes the sense of a normal, sane person within the natural attitude of other normal, sane persons, while simultaneously being aware of the dramaturgical imperative to control words and gestures in order to appear effectively to others. Failure in this delicate internal and external performance means being struck by an everyday version of stage fright or microphone panic in which a person forgets lines, loses the ability to act effectively, and actually experiences physiological reactions of panic and distress as he or she sweats, shakes, and gets red in the face and dry in the mouth. Common experiences of embarrassment test our poise, or the ability to be dramaturgically effective while remedying a threatened identity (Gross and Stone 1964).

Stigmatized persons necessarily learn to develop skill in handling problematic situations. And each of us is stigmatized in some way; each of us has faced problematic situations of our own or others' making; each of us has some modicum of skill at performing live and meeting the demands of the dramaturgical imperative. A sociological psychology of identity discusses mental patients, closet homosexuals, ethnics who pass, transsexuals who emerge, and the entire Goffmanesque coterie of spies, seducers, shills, and so on, because they constitute a constituency highly skilled in the universal human tasks of dramaturgical effectiveness. Those types of persons are explicitly skilled at what we all learn to do more or less well and without forethought; present, negotiate, and control multiple identities in a reasonable, organized hierarchy. To the extent that we all measure up to the dramaturgical imperative, we can get on with the business of living effectively with a sense of continuous self-identity amid the fragmentation of modern society.

The continuity of identity

The fact of multiple identities and the precariousness of meaning attached to any one identity in the situation raises the issue of continuity of personal identity. Continuity must be assured from situation to situation as a kind of "transsituational" identity to guarantee order, responsibility, and sanity. It is unthinkable to have a society in which individuals have no identity that remains the same across the many situations which comprise social reality and personal biography.

Identity must remain continuous across space as we move from place to place; it must somehow remain continuous across time as well. Individuals strive throughout life to sustain a sense of self sameness, or identity in the metaphysical sense of remaining always the same source of meaning, action, and experience. Biographical continuity is particularly difficult in modern society, compared with more fixed and simple societies (Erikson 1978). The modern person, for example, normally lives twice as long as people in previous historical periods. This simple biographical fact means that most people pass through middle age and many reach "old age" – a rare status in earlier periods. Thus, large numbers of individuals are likely to experience the deep realizations that in middle age, "I am not the same person I once was," or in old age, "I never became the person I wanted to be." These moving realizations are possible only on the assumption that each "I" in the sentence refers to the same person who believes totally in his or her experience of one continuous biography. If each "I" does not refer to the same person, then the sentence says nothing; it is nonsense.

The experience of identity continuity raises this question: What structures and processes sustain a sense of self sameness? There is no merely biological or simple cognitive answer that adequately guarantees the sense of personal continuity, though organic continuity and a continuous memory are required. Since identity is a socially constructed and symbolically sustained meaning, there must also be sociological psychological realities that guarantee the continuity of these meanings and allow us to construct and experience that crucial intimate meaning: that of my self as a continuous identity throughout all the changes which mark my life.

In the natural attitude and within routine situations, persons bracket, or typically are unaware of, the social production of their identities and of the concomitant self-awareness of an immediately available and undoubted sense of who they are. Deep doubts about identity are normally omitted from awareness. When they do intrude into our attention, life becomes uneasy, decisions become difficult, and disappointment or frustration begin to gnaw at our hearts.

The complexity and changeability of modern society put heavy strains on traditional carriers of identity continuity. There are effective traditional answers to the question: How is a sense of identity continuity naturally sustained? Traditional identities relied on stable and plausible social structures such as family and kinship; personal symbols such as an individual's name or the group's totem or territory; taken-for-granted interpretive procedures such as the conventional rules for doing gender, age, or occupation with unchallenged personal and social meaning; and transcendent myths or rituals identifying individuals in the cosmic scheme of reality and giving meaning to the great transitions in life, such as birth, puberty, marriage, old age, and death (Berger 1967; Luckmann 1967; Bellah 1968; Mol 1976). A sense of self sameness remained secure within traditional societies.

Consider, however, the degree of current change in the traditional structure of identity production and continuity: Family and the identities embodied in family relationships are changing in stability, composition, and cultural meaning (Weigert and Hastings 1977); personal names no longer carry the symbolic weight they did in traditionally oriented societies, since titular, totemic, religious, lineage, and ancestral meanings are weakened in the face of informal names, nicknames, faddish names, rationalized numbers, or bureaucratic "identities" on plastic cards; birth may involve two donors who are not parents; death may require a court order to "pull a plug"; the interpretive procedures and rules for doing gender, age, or occupation become the object of public debate and political conflict among interest groups representing different versions of such identities; and the transcendent myths and rituals are reduced to privatized meanings and ephemeral group identities offering therapeutic support, sectarian dominance, or collective submersion (Berger 1967; Schur 1976).

Over the life course, individuals now must rationally plan who they are going to be and seek the appropriate career line that institutionalizes the identity they desire. Biography is divided into careers, like lanes on a race track, some of which are blocked or truncated for different social groups. Every identity process from occupation to family is divided into careers (see Aldous 1978). Careers often do not carry their own intrinsic legitimation; we pursue a career as a means to something else, like money or success. Nor do careers normally give meaning to an entire life. The absence of a general and undoubted plausibility structure to support personal identity throughout life opened the way for a new sociocultural stage in the biography of moderns: the "mid-life crisis" (Gould 1972; Sheehy

1976; Erikson 1978; Levinson 1978). In the mid-life crisis, the meaning and continuity of identity is the focus of an interpretive imperative: How do we make sense out of our lives once we realize that our careers do not add up to a meaningful life? The modern is faced with the perennial question, only now the question is asked with full and explicit realization that there may be no answer other than the desiccation of grim stoicism or the exuberance of passionate romanticism.

At the situational level of everyday life, moderns manage a sense of identity continuity by more or less merging social roles and personal identities. Such a merger normally guarantees sufficient stability in self-presentation and others' responses to anchor the interactional flow of their lives, at least in the short run (McCall and Simmons 1978; Turner 1978). Over the life course, furthermore, individuals manage to sustain both memories of and aspirations for self that others are more or less able to sustain as well. The sequence of kin groups in the movement from family of orientation to family of procreation and on to family of gerontation is one such interactional chain underwriting a continuous memory of self. Cultural and biographical nostalgia is another source of continuity (Davis 1979). The universal issue of permanence and change in human meanings is acutely felt in the fervid modern quest for the continuity and centering of identity (Klapp 1969; cf. Burke 1965).

Identity and emotions

The rationality and abstracted bureaucratic organization of modern society create a new social context for human emotions. The felt need for identity continuity is one result. A highly rational and abstract context makes it difficult for moderns to give meaning to deep traditional or organic feelings. The abstract society desiccates and devalues feelings; it weakens the symbolism of emotions; it creates a collective search for a center of felt meaning. A cliché in modern thought is that many people suffer from emotional problems; they feel bad about themselves; they have lost the sensibility of moral feelings in a crush of callous indifference; or they are alienated from and out of touch with their own feeling selves. As we will be using the term, *emotion* refers to an organic feeling that as interpreted becomes a meaningful part of an individual's experience (Weigert 1983). Feelings, like any raw biological event, do not carry their own public or experiential definition. Such definitions are the work of culture; they are added to feelings and thereby transform raw feelings into interpreted and defined feelings that we know and experience as emotions (cf. Gordon 1981, who prefers "sentiment" to refer to socially constructed feelings).

Emotions manifest a person's deep relationship to the public and interactional domain of life (Hochschild 1975; Shott 1979; Finkelstein 1980). Changes in the meaning of emotional experience mark changes in the meaning of a person's life. Power and status relationships shape the emotions that structure our lives (Kemper 1978). As such, emotions provide rich, first-hand, and powerful content for the construction of identity. Whether a person wishes to or not, a surge of emotion becomes immediate evidence that she or he relates in that powerful way to self, another person or event, or a collectivity. We may not agree intellectually with a demogogue's message, and yet we may be moved in some inexplicable primitive way by the cadences of his harangue.

Prejudice driven by hatred, for example, tells a person how she or he relates to the target population before a word is ever spoken. The prejudiced, hating person is faced with the task of interpreting these emotions in such a way as to allow his or her other subjective and objective identities to remain plausible. How does a Christian who believes in the universal unity of all people in God's plan of human salvation reconcile this belief with an emotion which implies that some people are less human than others? How can a person claiming to be above animal impulses explain away that surge of ethnic prejudice which arises in spite of his or her intentions? There is a great deal of identity work to be done if that person ever hopes to integrate those emotions into the organization of his or her identities. And they should be integrated.

The alternative of ignoring strong emotions and failing to make sense out of them is a dangerous tactic. Unintegrated emotions may become fixed or cathected in ways that pose an even greater threat to a meaningful self-identity than the effort at integration itself. At the very least, ignored emotions deprive a person of a possible source of meaning from the powerful realm of human feelings. After all, to the extent that a part of a person's emotional life is meaningless and unintegrated, so too is part of that person's identity, since emotions are part of our constructed identities. The search for human "sensitivity" that lies behind widespread social movements for increased self-awareness and greater interpersonal intimacy is a collective attempt to define as meaningful emotions raw feelings which moderns cannot easily handle.

Individuals who have undergone deeply moving experiences seek group support for getting control of those feelings. Soldiers returning from the Vietnam war, for example, struggle to make sense of the profound feelings they experience as powerful "rage." Their rage arises out of viscerally moving but socially senseless feelings experienced in the face of death, suffering, and brutality in fighting what they see as a meaningless war for an uncomprehending and unsympathetic society (Lifton 1976). Veterans returning from battle and filled with unintelligible rage experience problems in living a "normal" life when they return to a "home" in which they no longer feel at home. They need a way to interpret and integrate their deep feelings into meaningful emotions and thus to reestablish a livable link between their self-identity and the public meanings available in contemporary America. Returnees from the Peace Corps, hostages from long captivity, or others who have deep experiences of different cultures face similar problems in the emotional realignment of identities when they return home. Emotional ''at-homeness'' must be constructed and sustained, like any other dimension of identity.

Summary

This chapter presents an effort to outline a theory of identity in incipient propositional form. Building on symbolic interaction and neo-phenomenological writings, we presented a series of statements we think show promise for the systematic development of a coherent framework for investigating the complex central issue of human identity. The definition of identity suggested at the end of the propositional presentation, we hope, will stimulate others to work the phenomenon ever more adequately. Finally, we touched briefly upon five themes surrounding identity from the level of philosophical anthropology to that of sociohistorical forms of identity and the crucial issue of human emotions. The following chapters attempt partial applications and extensions of identity theory to substantive areas such as gender, and prenatal and postmortem identity.

PART II

So what? Applying and extending identity theory, and back to society

True to the strategy of pragmatic social constructionist identity theory, we carry the project another step along the way from generic theory to the turf of empirical grounding. Objectivated social reality, although largely formed and continually re-formed through patterned and/or meaningful human action, takes on the characteristics of "things." As such, objectivated social reality ought to be interrogated with whatever methods and data the questions informing the investigation require. The crux, as we mentioned, is knowing how to interpret the methods, the data, and the links among them and the original reality under investigation. Part II presents two examples of such interrogation – namely, the formulation of a middle-range theory, and a speculative extension of identity theory. These efforts are not full-fledged articulations of, or rigorously deduced propositions from, identity theory. Rather, they are in the order of feasibility studies and suggestive extensions. They begin to show what identity as a sensitizing concept and our generic theory may offer to sociological psychologists.

Chapter 3 selects propositions from the incipient theory and applies them to the substantive area linking identities and bodies – namely, gender identity. After discussing gender as a socially constructed identity, the chapter further specifies the issue by moving toward a more limited empirical domain, the link between a specific gender identity and occupation. At this point, the discussion moves out of the social constructionist stance and into standard theory-building tactics. Focusing on persons with a homosexual identity, middle-range testable propositions linking homosexuality and occupational characteristics are formulated and interrelated.

Chapter 4 attempts to take identity theory and extend it to new subject matter – namely, identities without typical bodies. It seems reasonable, though not all that obvious, that if identity in some of its modes is a totally social construction, then we should be able to apply identity theory to a relatively untouched and perhaps unpromising phenomenon – to the reality of identities without fully interacting bodies or any bodies at all. Interpretation of the meanings of such phenomena as preconception, or prenatal, and postmortem identities serves as a kind of *experimentum crucis* demonstrating the power, validity, and fruitfulness of a pragmatic social constructionist paradigm of human identity. Identities without bodies are not phantoms; rather, they are pieces of purely social reality.

Finally, in Chapter 5 we briefly recapitulate the journey to identity theory and the main contours of our tentative but we hope suggestive attempts to ground the theory over more or less empirical terrains. A final word reiterates what we take to be the original impetus to the emergence of identity – namely, that it is a central concept and crucial issue for those living in a complex, changing, and especially culturally democratic society. Identity is one of the themes that define our time on the stage of history.

3. Applying identity theory to bodies: gender identity

Relationships among various identities is fruitfully addressed by the incipient identity theory we are developing. This chapter builds selectively on Chapter 2, delineates the major concepts and definitions that are the focus of attention throughout the discussion, further grounds identity theory by applying it to gender, and attempts a middle-range theory relating homosexuality and occupation. With identity as the focus, we illustrate the fruitfulness and scope of identity theory by a dual movement of analysis: toward the self through a discussion of transsexuality, and toward status and institutions through an attempt at a middle-range theory.

Categories of identity

For purposes of this chapter, the foci of identity can be divided into personal, group, and social categories. Mol (1976, 1978) presented these foci in terms of an *identity continuum*. The concept of a continuum is misleading, however, for it connotes a hierarchical relationship among his ''levels'' of identity. A more practical conceptualization is to consider different identities as falling into categories, with the criterion for categorization being the source from which the identity is constructed. In addition, the categories of identities are interrelated, either because they are in conflict due to their differentiating aspects, or because they are congruous based on their integrative capacity. Not only does this simple schema provide a general view of how identities can be categorized, it is an analytical tool for showing how personal identities are expressed at other levels. It is possible to exemplify the relationships by choosing one or two forms of personal identity and showing the links between them and different group identities with respect to integrative and differentiating characteristics.

The focus of this chapter is gender identity. To begin our discussion, we must make distinctions often masked in the general literature between gender, sex, and sexual identities. Normally, *gender identity* is dichotomized into male and female types of persons, while *sexual identity* is differentiated into several types of sexual interaction: heterosexual, homosexual (male), lesbian (female), or bisexual (Kessler and McKenna 1978); Petras 1978). Sociologists have emphasized the importance of distinguishing *sex identity* from both sexual and gender identities. The first is biological and the last two are social constructions, though in the natural attitude of everyday life, two or three of these identities are often seen as one and attributed to a single source or explanation, such as hormones or anatomy.

We are actually concerned with three different but interrelated identities: sex, gender, and sexual. Sex identity is based on biological criteria of genetic and physiological classifications, such as the presence of male or female genitals, or male XY or female XX chromosomal configurations. Gender identity refers to internalized sociocultural meanings and expectations that accompany the normal sense of maleness or femaleness taken for granted in society (Kessler and Mc-Kenna 1978; Petras 1978; Ponse 1978). Sexual identity "refers to one's social and/or personal identity in terms of preference for sexual activity with a particular gender. . . . These identities are generally presumed to be stable over the life span" (Ponse 1978:27). When sexual identity is interpreted in a social context, it is commonly associated with sexual activity (behavioral modes) and objects of sexual choice, such as heterosexual male–female, homosexual male–male or female–female, or bisexual relationships. All three of these personal identities are interactive; each influences the others in terms of their definitions and implications for the individual's position and meaning to self and others.

Gender and sex: social construction versus biological determinism

A fundamental ambiguity that hinders an adequate understanding of human identity is the lack of a firm distinction between gender and sex identities. Often the terms are used synonymously when referring to a particular category or status of individuals. In our everyday lives, we refer to sex roles, sex identities, sex stereotypes, and sexism, thus implying that a person's sex can be firmly and easily distinguished and is the relevant category for interpreting social reality. We also live in a world of two "sexes" of male and female. This dichotomy of sex is regarded as indisputable in our society. But what are the bases for categorizing an individual as man/woman, male/female, or masculine/feminine?

The traditional biological view holds that the distinction is based on a "biological imperative," that certain differences exist between the sex "male" and the sex "female" which are biologically determined through genetic composition, hormonal properties, and the configuration of genitalia (Money and Ehrhardt 1972). Those differences are then extended to include attributes and behaviors thought to be characteristic of the category of each sex. In other words, if one is born of the fe/male sex, s/he is biologically predisposed to become passive/aggressive, nurturant/dominant, and emotional/unemotional (Petras 1978). The individual will then internalize a male or female sex identity and sustain sex roles consistent with the characteristics that have been biologically determined for him or her. Until recently, this imperative has been perpetuated under the assumption that biological differences are universal, inevitable, and desirable, and that they justify and explain the social inequality of the sexes (Lambert 1978). Extremists in the reemerging field of sociobiology have based their position in the scientific world on the premise that biology is destiny. In the past decade, however, extensive research has shown that many of the biologically based behavioral differences which were taken for granted, such as male aggressiveness and female passivity, are not absolutes (Holter 1970; Gagnon and Simon 1973; Kaplan and Bean 1976; Sargent 1977; Lambert 1978).

As a result of these studies, sociological psychologists contend that sex and gender terms confuse basic issues if they are used interchangeably to indicate differences among individuals. Extensive research supports the claim that gender is a separate role or identity that can be attributed to an individual regardless of biologically determined sex (Stoller 1968; Walum 1977; Chafetz 1978; Jaggar and Struhl 1978).

Considering aspects of identity, Petras (1978:96) discusses how gender identity is a natural internalization and behavioral consequence of biological sex assignment; and he offers the following definitions to distinguish between the two:

. . . use the word *sex* to refer to the fact of a *biological* basis and distinctiveness, i.e., being born either male or female. . . . The word *gender,* however, refers to *socially* learned responses, meanings, and cues that are taken as reflections of society's conceptions of masculinity and femininity. Sex, being biological, is linked to the body. Gender, as a constellation of meanings concerning self definitions and behavior toward others, serves as a framework within which we are able to interpret the responses of our bodies; gender becomes linked to the body through socially learned meanings. (italics his)

Reflecting on this relationship, Ponse (1978:25) notes that "Gender identity, the experienced sense of maleness or femaleness, is based on sex assignment at birth. It is the inner sense of being male or female – corresponding with the body's form and structure." These considerations lead to a social constructionist view of gender.

To illustrate the social construction of gender identity, Oakley (1972) and Stoller (1968) point to cases of sexual ambiguities and gender identity formation. These cases indicate that

. . . a child can achieve a firm gender identity as a male even if he lacks the prime insignia of maleness, a penis. The child senses that gender is not necessarily defined by sex. . . . Mostly the social situation defines gender (wife = woman, dentist = man, and so on) or gender is visible as a sum of qualities, including mannerism, way of speaking, dress, choice of topics in conversation and so on. Gender is a visible fact most of the time: sex is not. (Oakley 1972:161)

In looking at the relationship between identity and role, Money and Ehrhardt (1972:4) define gender identity as the

. . . sameness, unity, and persistence of one's individuality as a male, female, or ambivalent, in greater or lesser degree, especially as it is experienced in self-awareness and behavior; gender identity is the private experience of the gender role, and the gender role is the public expression of gender identity.

To this, Ponse (1978:26) adds that "Gender identity implies a whole series of expectations and meanings with respect to gender role and sexual identities." Kessler and McKenna (1978:10), as well as Stoller (1968) make a further distinction between gender identity and "gender-role identity" that "refers to how much a person approves of and participates in feelings and behaviors, which are seen as 'appropriate' for his/her gender." Finally, Davidson and Gordon (1979:13) differentiate between gender identity and gender role by noting that identity is the "idealized" aspect of the "awareness that one is a boy or that one is a girl; it includes an understanding that one's maleness or femaleness is a permanent trait." Gender role, on the other hand, refers to expectations associated with "the common role enactment of behavior attached to that identity."

Garfinkel (1967) and Kessler and McKenna (1978) emphasize that research and literature have failed to distinguish deeply enough between biological "sex" and cultural or social "gender." The latter cite studies that attempt to explain the differences between men and women, and criticize researchers for continuing to perpetuate the myth that sex and gender are inseparable qualities of an individual.

This brief review of the literature concludes that gender is a distinct quality of an individual which is socially and culturally defined in the domains of identity, role, and status. And if gender is a social construction of reality in everyday life, then the next step is to determine the rules by which gender is recognized and attributed to an individual. We can analyze gender from a sociological-psychological perspective to illustrate the validity and fruitfulness of identity theory.

In order to conceptualize gender as a constructed type in an individual's identity set, we need to locate gender as a dimension of the self. Initially, we call attention to the "genesis of the self" as formulated by Mead (1934) and outlined in Meltzer (1964). By considering the construction of the gender male or female as specific examples, the stages of development of the self are illustrated. For instance, in the "play" stage, a child/girl will actually play the role of mother/woman and will begin to form a self/female. In the "game" stage, the child/boy will come to view the intentions and expectations of a generalized other/male and internalize the definitions of the generalized role/masculine.

Similarly, gender can be interpreted as a dimension of self by virtue of certain basic concepts that have come to define it specifically as such. Gender identity is a kind of *self*-attribution (Kessler and McKenna 1978). Petras claims that "Gender identity allows us to make sense out of ourselves as neutral objects in a symbolic environment" (1978:97). Also, the location of gender as "self" can be found in Chafetz (1978). In her section on "The Bringing Up of Dick and Jane," she specifically cites the work of Mead and Cooley in explaining how an individual's gender identity emerges.

Gender identity, negotiation, and validation

Gender attribution and gender accomplishment imply a process of negotiation. In other words, gender is socially constructed because:

1. Society makes the attribution based on biological and/or gender cues.
2. Individuals engage in artful impression management in order to warrant the attribution of gender.

Thus, there is a dialectic among the impressions an individual hopes to foster, the expressions he or she actually gives off, and the perceptions and interpretations of others, all couched in the situated meanings surrounding an interaction. Utilizing Goffman's (1959) dramaturgical approach, we see that "presenting gender" is equally important in allowing an audience to engage in the attribution process.

The distinctive feature of dramaturgy as a variation of symbolic interactionism is the premise that "when human beings interact each desires to 'manage' the impressions the others receive of him/her. In effect, each puts on a 'show' for the others" (Meltzer et al. 1975:68). The necessary ingredients of Goffman's approach include an actor who engages in a performance while making use of settings and props for the benefit of an audience. Through the performance, the actor strives to manage the impressions the audience has of the character as a personal reality in their lives.

At the core of this approach is the self as object; namely, that through the performance, the actor attempts to foster an impression of a self. Furthermore, the self wishes to make a presentation that leads to a positive outcome in terms of self's own intentions. As Meltzer et al. (1975:68–9) point out: "The outcome of each performance is an imputation by the audience of a particular kind of self to the performed character(s). . . . . It is to the individual's advantage, of course, to present himself/herself in ways that will best serve his/her ends." This object is experienced as an identity in various modes of presentation, negotiation, and validation.

Gender identity and transsexualism

Given that gender is a social category constructed on biological organisms that usually are sexually dimorphic, certain rules must exist by which members of society engage in the process of giving and sustaining a gender identity. The methods by which those rules are formulated and applied have been studied by ethnomethodologists. The most notable works to date are Garfinkel's (1967) case study of Agnes, and the research of Kessler and McKenna (1978) on transsexuals – in particular, Rachel. The Kessler and McKenna work receives primary attention here.

The argument for gender identity as a social construction rests on the primacy of gender attribution, or the "active process, based on information received, and involving implicit rules for assigning characteristics" relevant to the maleness or femaleness of an individual (1978:18). The contention is that information presented on gender assignment, gender identity, and gender role does not provide an accurate gender attribution because there is never enough data to interpret. Yet once a gender attribution is made, other gender-related information can be interpreted and applied to fill in the individual's identity. The process of attributing gender is a primary act of imposing identities for categorizing individuals.

This process should not be confused with attribution theory in social psychology found in the works like Jones et al. (1971), which is concerned with attributing causality to behavior based on the perception of the other's actions. Thus, the three elements of attribution theory are as follows:

1.   Was the act observed?
2.   Was the act intended? and
3.   Was the act coerced?

(See Shaver 1975 for a full discussion of attribution theory.) Kessler and McKenna (1978:18) contend that attribution theory "does not concern itself with the deep structure of social interaction. It is concerned with the conditions under which people assign motives, traits, characteristics, etc. to others on the basis of limited information. . . ." They believe that attribution theory has not been concerned with the gender-attribution process itself. The objective of the Kessler and McKenna study, therefore, was to review previous work on gender, to demonstrate how scientific treatment of gender is grounded in everyday gender attribution, and to present some research findings on gender attribution in everyday life.

The particular method Kessler and McKenna used to examine gender attribution was fashioned after Garfinkel's study of Agnes, a male-to-female transsexual. The phenomenon of transsexualism is chosen because it is considered to the "richest source of information on gender as a social construction" (1978:xi). In other words, the transsexual presents a unique situation because a social contradiction exists between the biological sex and the gender identity of the individual. A transsexual can successfully "pass"; that is, be socially accepted in the identity that he or she intends in a gender role that is inconsistent with biological "sex" and yet conforms with expectations about gender identity.

Because the notion of passing is integral to our analysis, we will qualify our use of the concept. *Passing* commonly means to be taken for something or someone that a person really is not. A light-skinned black who attempts to be taken for a white person is considered to be passing as white. In our analysis, we do *not* imply that a person is really not what he or she appears to be. We believe that in the most basic events of everyday life, everyone is passing, or is doing something in an effort to be taken as he or she intends beyond what is actually realized.

Ethnomethodological studies of transsexuals attempt to discover the rules by which society attributes gender under the condition of passing (see Garfinkel 1967:122–128, 137–45; Kessler and McKenna 1978:113–14, 126–36). Garfinkel studied Agnes in order to document the rules for continuous gender accomplishment in everyday interaction. He presents several objective rules that form the natural attitude in Western society toward gender:

1. There are two and only two genders.
2. Every individual must be classified as being one gender or the other.
3. A gender is invariant.
4. Any exception to the gender dichotomy is considered to be abnormal or pathological.
5. There are no transfers between genders.
6. Genitals represent the essential sign of a gender.
7. The gender dichotomy is natural and exists independent of any scientific or other criteria.
8. Being male or female is also natural and is not dependent on anyone else's evaluation.

Garfinkel investigated what happens to the taken-for-granted assumptions when there are violations of the interpretive rules. Agnes, as a transsexual, violated rules 3, 5, and 6 of the natural attitude. Yet those rules, if bracketed, point to the fact that the need to pass as a certain sex actually reinforces the existence of the natural attitude by showing how the transsexual and others make sense of the gender reality in spite of the contradictory biological cues. Kessler and McKenna (1978:114) note this paradox:

The transsexual produces a sense of facticity of gender in social interactions in the same way everyone produces it. The natural attitude allows no exceptions, so the transsexual, an apparent exception, is seen as not an exception after all, but rather an example of the "objective" truth of the facts.

Garfinkel was concerned with how Agnes was able to "do" gender, the process by which she was able to produce a sense of the real objective facts even though she exemplifies how those facts are not always true – that is, consistent with another presumably more "natural" reality, such as biological fact. By recording the successful accomplishment of a new gender identity by transsexuals, his study of Agnes reveals some of the taken-for-granted rules operating in everyday interactions.

In their more elaborate study of transsexuals, Kessler and McKenna did not place the same emphasis on process as Garfinkel, although similar conclusions were reached – that gender for the transsexual must be accomplished, and the passing of a transsexual reinforces the presence of a natural attitude toward gender. The significance of their research lies in its contribution to understanding the structural dimensions of gender attribution.

They report on a study in which two ambiguous body figures were overlaid with transparencies depicting various genital, physiological, and clothing arrangements. From the patterns of respondents' attributions of gender identity to the body figures at different stages of the overlay, Kessler and McKenna generated an incipient theory of gender. Briefly stated, they found that respondents make gender attributions by looking for male cues. In the absence of a significant number of male cues, a female gender attribution is made. This implies that the male gender typification dominates individual perceptions, so that females are "nonmale" derivations of the everyday construction of gender identity. The theory begins to provide the tools or characteristics necessary for accurate gender attribution and to unpack the deep assumptions underlying an individual's and a society's construction of gender as a social reality. Garfinkel's study, on the other hand, highlights the interactional processes in operation during gender accomplishment.

The overall conclusion of the ethnomethodological studies is that gender is socially constructed according to rules, interpretive procedures, and interactional processes we are now beginning to document and understand. This construction is the product of, and has an impact upon, the situated meanings, cultural rules, and social processes that allow for the presenting and coding of gender. Consequently, the ultimate goal of passing for transsexuals is to ensure that gender cues socially presented will conform to the natural attitude and its real, objective facts so that a "correct" gender attribution can be made.

Presenting gender identity

For most of us in everyday life, presenting gender is not a problem. We were given a gender assignment at birth based on unambiguous biological cues, have assumed and internalized a consistent gender identity based on a congruous gender attribution, and perform appropriate gender roles on a daily basis. In other words, all the genes, hormones, genitals, feelings, expectations, and cultural rules for being gender-male or gender-female routinely combine to form the deep-dimension self experienced as the socially real man or woman. The predicament of the transsexual, especially the preoperative one, provides a rich example of how an individual engages in artful impression management to present a problematic gender identity as beyond doubt and within a totally taken-for-granted world of social action. The technique described by Goffman serves as a model for illustrating the management of impressions in concrete situations, and transsexualism provides the material for discussion.

As Goffman (1959:212) points out in his chapter on the art of impression management:

In order to prevent the occurrence of incidents and the embarrassment consequent upon them, it will be necessary for all the participants in the interaction, as well as those who do not participate, to possess certain attributes and to express these attributes in practices employed for saving the show.

He defines these practices as being of three kinds:

1. Defensive measures used by a performer to save his or her own show
2. Protective measures used by the audience and outsiders to assist the performer in saving the show
3. Measures of "tact regarding tact" the performer must take in order to allow the audience and outsiders to employ their own protective measures

We extend Goffman's understanding and use of these practices by applying them to the transsexual in concrete situations.

Under the first category, Goffman refers to three dramaturgical attributes: loyalty, discipline, and circumspection. Agnes represents the case in which these attributes were successfully displayed in order to succeed in her gender performance. She was able to conceal the fact that she was taking female hormones in order to validate her other biological "deformities" and have them surgically corrected, which is indicative of her loyalty to her gender identity and character, or feelings of always being a "female." Her discipline to her gender identity is exemplified by how consistently she presented the same part to the researchers with a high level of intellectual and emotional involvement, just as her circumspection was illustrated by her choice of audience (Garfinkel and Stoller, a professional sociologist and a physician, respectively) who would remain loyal to her presented identity and support the staging of her show. She laid out the ground rules by writing her own script; that is, not allowing the staff to research her past or interview her mother. She was thus allowed to keep her audience disciplined within the performance she designed.

Rachel can be viewed as displaying these attributes more in terms of a social rather than a research audience. We learn of situations that arose in a variety of contexts during which her gender identity was put to the test. These events include her visit to a license bureau for the purpose of changing the name and sex on her driver's license, and her encounter with a department store clerk over making a name change on her credit card. Through her accounts, we are made aware of his–her gradual biological transformation and gender socialization over a period of several years. As a result, her social performance takes shape more as a carefully designed script that we assume she followed in her everyday interactions.

The second category Goffman identifies involves the protective measures used by the audience in support of the performance. We refer to the various passing rituals in which each performer had to engage, and look at the roles that Garfinkel/Stoller and Kessler/McKenna played in helping their subjects through the transitions (in addition to other audiences and their impact on the performance). In terms of passing, both Agnes and Rachel had to perform socially as females in order to achieve and make secure their rights to live in the elected sex status while providing for the possibility of detection and ruin (Garkinfel 1967:118). In the Goffmanesque sense, they assumed the role of actors engaging in a serious and precarious performance, since biologically they were both still males, and using settings and props for the benefit of an audience in order to portray their female gender identity. Both studies are rich with examples of the protective practices undertaken to facilitate the performance of Rachel and Agnes as female-gendered persons who also possessed a male sex identity. For instance, the audience for Agnes employed protective practices by not probing into her past, not interviewing her mother, and diagnosing her "male" sex identity as a biological deformity. Rachel's audience also employed such practices by making the name and gender pronoun change at her request prior to surgery.

The final tactic Goffman discusses concerns the measures the performer must take to allow the audience and outsiders to be protective. The performer must be sensitive to his or her audience so that they are able to protect the show – what Goffman (1959:234) refers to as "tact with respect to tact." Such second-order tact avoids embarrassment or inopportune intrusions that could jeopardize the performance and thereby discredit the character and identity for both actor and audience.

The purpose of tact regarding tact is closely related to the avoidance of stigma. Goffman (1963) describes two types of stigma, external and internal, both of which are potentially discrediting to the performer's presented identity. Feinbloom (1976) uses the notion of stigma to illustrate how the transsexual engages in the daily performance of gender identity in order to conceal externally visible stigmas as physically discrepant cues, and internally hidden stigmas such as an incident in the person's biography that would discredit the currently performed identity. In effect, the possibility of stigma presents a double threat to the transsexual, in that a poor performance can produce stigma in two dimensions:

1. The stigma that is attached to the discredited performance itself
2. The stigma that accompanies the labeling of the actor as a transsexual, with all the concomitant traits typically associated with the label

Kessler and McKenna develop four areas that contribute to the process of gender attribution: general talk, public appearance, the private body, and talk about the personal past (1978:127). Here the emphasis is more on the content of the process of gender attribution. The authors treat everyday gender construction as a performance through displays of characteristics, or structural determinants, typically associated with a particular gender. This is in addition to the employment of situational strategies (like Garfinkel's processes) to protect the displays that are intended to construct and sustain a gender identity.

This discussion has focused on the interrelationship between gender identity and transsexualism. We have shown the applicability of identity theory to the life experiences and interactional situations of the transsexual. Particular emphasis is placed on how gender identity affects the strategies employed by the transsexual in order to pass successfully. In the next section, we turn to the relationship between gender identity and homosexuality with respect to their influences in the occupational realm. Our analysis illustrates the wider applicability of identity theory and its utility for understanding phenomena in a structural context such as occupation.

Gender identity, homosexuality, and occupation

The choice of gender and sexual identities as objects for analysis in an occupational context has particular significance. As Mol (1976:156) notes: "The strongly unifying character of sexuality makes it an appropriate source of integrative symbolism on any level, whether social, group, or personal." The integrative function of successful gender identity with appropriate objects of sexual choice is a deep structure of meaning in society. Ponse (1978:27) states that the only sexual identity that is widely supported in Western culture is heterosexuality; in fact, the heterosexual identity of social actors is normally taken for granted. She notes, however, that sexual identity can be individualistic and idiosyncratic, as exemplified in the presentations of homosexuality, lesbianism, and bisexuality. The presence of these other forms of identities questions the integrative nature of sexuality in the symbolic meaning system recognized in gender-pluralistic societies, or in societies in which no ideology dominates the public domain. On this issue, Mol (1976:156–7) states:

Positive codes, as well as negative taboos, operate in most societies, and make plain the importance of the harmonious interaction between the sacralization of self (and often sexual fulfillment) and sacralization of social identity (and often sexual restraint). Regulation does not mean prohibition. This combination of positive codes and negative taboos in particular societies is usually a very good indication as to where the sensitive division between personal and social identity is drawn.

In Western society, there is a positive code for heterosexual activity which, for those with a heterosexual personal identity, leads to assumed sexual fulfillment. There is an ideological consistency between normative expectations, sexual behavior, and personal fulfillment for the self. There are also negative taboos regarding sexual identity in the areas of homosexuality and bisexuality, in addition, of course, to sanctions against other forms of sexual behavior that are clinically and typically defined as pathological. Formal or legal codes as well as informal networks have developed for regulating sexual activity in these areas. Certain state, county, and municipal legislative bodies have enacted laws specifically prohibiting public displays of nonheterosexual or "deviant" behaviors; others allow discrimination in the areas of housing, employment, and other economic or social realms against those who violate the taboos (Humphreys 1972; Harry and DeVall 1978; Ponse 1978).

In the area of informal sanctions, the reactions to expressed homosexuality can be described in terms of Goffman's (1963) analysis of stigmatization. Ponse focuses her discussion of secrecy in the lesbian world to underscore the potential for stigma and the mechanisms used for its avoidance. She states: "[A] secret society tends to arise under conditions of public 'unfreedom' when legal or normative proscriptions regarding persons or behavior necessitate the protectiveness of secrecy" (1978:57). Secrecy becomes a central tactic because it underlies the presentation–negotiation–validation process in the case of severely stigmatized persons. As we have argued, however, normals are engaged in the same process, because all have some discrediting information relevant to at least some identities. Therefore, secrecy control is a universal feature of everyday life that becomes centrally important in the cases of transsexuals and homosexuals.

Such control is typically achieved through primary group affiliations. Simmel (1950) delineates both the function and the limitations of primary groups as secret societies. On the one hand, it can be said that primary groups serve the function of secret societies to the extent that they are characterized by extensive and intensive intimacy, integration through a common bond or reciprocity of goals, and degree of formality, which is usually slight (Rose 1980). The formation of a primary group is based on high degrees of intimacy and integration. Despite the fact that informal, secretive groups of homosexuals emerge due to their collective and perceived need for intimacy and invisibility, members continue to maintain a certain distance and reserve from each other that is often not totally overcome in even the most intimate of homosexual primary groups.

American culture operates on the heterosexual assumption that parties to an interaction in a straight setting are assumed to be heterosexual unless some indication of nonheterosexuality is given (Ponse 1978). This assumption is, furthermore, based on a principle of consistency: A congruent and coherent relationship is assumed to exist for sex assignment, gender role, gender identity, and sexual object of choice. Jaggar and Struhl (1977:162) state that ". . . individuals are engendered in order that marriage can be guaranteed. Levi-Strauss comes dangerously close to saying that heterosexuality is an instituted process." Once institutionalization occurs, it becomes more difficult for an individual to violate the natural attitude and heterosexual assumption without risking public stigmatization.

As a result of the exigency and power of the assumption of heterosexuality and the principle of consistency, the nonheterosexual becomes a potential object for stigma or negative imagery. Thus, the real or perceived need for secrecy of one's "gayness" results from both the fear of stigma and the hostility nonheterosexuals expect from the straight world. To avoid discovery, the homosexual employs strategies such as posing as one who is straight either through language or marital "fronts," restriction of gay activities to prevent disclosure, separation of public and private activities and associations, and counterfeit secrecy of the true nature of homosexual liaisons in order to limit disclosure to those within the homosexual subculture (Ponse 1978:59–74). These strategies can be interpreted as some form of passing, as described previously in this chapter and in the work of ethnomethodologists (Garfinkel 1967; Kessler and McKenna 1978).

"Passers" are caught in the dilemma of sexual identity dissonance: In conforming to the heterosexual assumption, they create a contradiction between personal sexual identity and social gender identity. This particular form of identity crisis is discussed below. First, however, we outline the categories of identity specific to the homosexual in terms of our consonance–dissonance dichotomy,

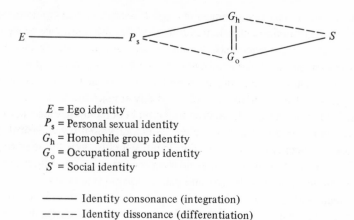

E = Ego identity
P_s = Personal sexual identity
G_h = Homophile group identity
G_o = Occupational group identity
S = Social identity

——— Identity consonance (integration)
– – – – Identity dissonance (differentiation)

Figure 3.1   Interrelationships among categories of identity. Note that an additional identity, organizational identity, was introduced in Chapter 2. For the present analysis, organizational identity is considered to be an intervening structural variable between G_h or G_o and S, and will not be used as a separate category here.

which allows us to explore those categories of identity and their interrelationships that are problematic for the homosexual attempting anonymity in a straight society.

In developing Mol's (1976) general framework, we expand on the relationship between the personal sexual identity of the homosexual and other group or social identities. Figure 3.1 depicts these relationships.

The first category, ego identity *(E)*, represents the composite personality of the individual from which the personal sexual identity *(P_s)* emerges. As we noted in Chapter 2, the use of the term "ego" becomes problematic within sociological psychology because of the variety of connotations and denotations in use. The psychoanalytic model uses ego to refer to the executive agent of personality, "the locus of perception, evaluation, anticipation, and decision," the function of which is to "remain in touch with reality, to take note of changing conditions, to seize opportunities for gratification and security. . . ." (Wheelis 1958:98). More consistent with the interactionist tradition is Goffman's (1963) conceptualization of ego as a totally subjective, "felt identity," in contrast to personal and social identities.

The problem with these definitions is that the first places too much emphasis on the rational nature of ego, while the latter overlooks the synthesizing character of ego and its impact as a functioning, integrative force. A formulation that appears to bridge the gap is offered by Erikson (1968:211), who suggests that identity formation has two components: a self aspect and an ego aspect. Ego-identity results from the synthesizing function of the individual "environmental" frontier of the ego, whereas self-identity grasps social reality. Consequently, "One can then speak of ego identity when one discusses the ego's synthesizing power in the light of its central psychosocial function, and of self-identity when the integration of the individual's self- and role-images are under discussion." This dual synthesis is a continual process throughout the individual's life course.

The second category of identity in the model is personal sexual identity (P_s), which is one aspect of ego-identity. This identity is closely tied to sex and gender identities, because the latter serve as the primary criteria for definitions of sexual identity. As noted previously, sex and gender identities are major links between an individual and society. In American society, heterosexuality is the taken-for-granted sexual identity. A "normal" person would be a biological male or female, who has a corresponding masculine or feminine gender identity, and who selects the opposite sex as preferred objects of sexual choice.

For homosexuals, sex, sexual, and gender identities are not congruent or integrated; there is dissonance. And this dissonance may be internal or external. Internal dissonance is exemplified by the case of a homosexual purposively passing as straight. If such a performance is successful, there will be external consonance despite the lack of internal identity integration. There can also be external dissonance, or tension in social relationships, between different identities in interactional settings. An example would be the dissonance that may arise when a homosexual goes public, thereby violating both the assumption of heterosexuality and the principle of consistency. Yet the creation of this external dissonance may ultimately lead to internal consonance for the individual because she or he has satisfied personal sexual identification needs. We will focus mainly on this external dissonance as we develop a middle-range theory linking homosexual personal identity with occupational group identity.

The relationship between gender and personal sexual identity requires elaboration. It is the recognition of dissonance between these identities, coupled with an awareness of the heterosexual assumption and the principle of consistency, that motivates the nonheterosexual to resort to secretive strategies to avoid stigma. The personal homosexual identity may be known, suspected, or even rejected by the individual through some rationalization or disclaiming process (Ponse 1978). If rejected, eventual acceptance may result from an ascriptive process brought on by extended interaction and labeling. Regardless of whether the sexual identity is congruent with or contradicts cultural expectations, personal sexual identity is a symbolically significant component of the human condition.

The third type of identity with which the personal sexual identity is interrelated is group identity. For this analysis, two group identities are selected as significant for the situation of the homosexual. The first group (G_h) is the cluster of homophile organizations that serve as a means for homosexuals to express their sexual preference. They act as primary groups for homosexuals, where personal sexual identity can be openly acknowledged. Such groups can be categorized into four types, depending upon the major aims of their activities:

1. The activists that overtly seek social change through collective effort
2. The social or recreational organizations that serve as an outlet without stigma or negative sanctioning, and that are structured and socially visible, but less concerned with changing cultural biases against homosexuals
3. The educational organizations that seek to counsel homosexuals and/or the general public in an effort to destigmatize nonheterosexual activity
4. Less visible informal networks

As indicated in Figure 3.1, the relationship between personal sexual identity and homophile group identity is typically one of consonance. Membership in homophile groups serves to integrate the identities in both categories, because the nature of the relationship between personal sexual and group identities is mutual support. As Ponse (1978:92) found:

All gay groups within the gay subculture serve certain general functions that support the identities of their members, including changing the meanings of the category lesbian through *normalization* of the lesbian world, *nihilation* of the straight world, provision of *ideological justifications* for lesbianism, and *aristocratization* of lesbianism in the face of stigma. (italics in the original)

Through these strategies, homophile groups attempt to neutralize the stigmatizing effects of public judgments and to overcome public prejudice. Affiliation with homophile organizations strengthens the gay liberation movement by demonstrating the size and composition of the nonheterosexual population. This increased visibility is intended to facilitate laws to prevent discrimination against the gay community (Levine 1979). As a result, the relationship between personal homosexual identity and homophile group identity is not only consonant for the most part, but reciprocal in terms of goal orientation. The relationship is also paradoxical to some extent. Homosexuals who attempt to retreat from a societal stigma are thrust into homophile "aristocratization." This exchange of one cultural source of identity validation for another, which is taken to be more noble and formidable, serves as a powerful example of the social construction of the meaning of gender at work in the face of a negative generalized other.

The other group identity that we selected is occupational identity (G_o). Sex and gender identities are significant links between individual and the social structure via occupational roles and their concomitant systems of power and trust. Sexual identity can become a primary issue if a homosexual identity becomes known or suspected when considering occupation and work performance. If the work setting is typically a straight environment operating on the heterosexual assumption, occupational identity and work performance become secondary to the importance of sexual identity, with the former being reevaluated and reinterpreted once a homosexual identity is suspected or confirmed (Humphreys 1972; Ponse 1978; Levine 1979). The awareness context, or acknowledgement of identity information known about each member, is a key issue (see Glaser and Strauss 1964), and is also a primary factor in the extent to which dissonance and consonance are internally or externally felt by the individual.

There are two dimensions of G_o identity. One is the sociological psychological aspect of occupational identity, or the definition of self that a particular occupation has for others with whom the individual interacts. The second is the organizational or sociocultural dimension from which an occupational identity develops. In effect, any occupation encompasses two levels of reality: the interactional and the institutional/societal. Although it is the former with which we are most concerned in our analysis of the relationships among categories of identity, the latter must be acknowledged as the source from which those meanings are primarily derived.

To illustrate the research implications of applying identity theory to the occupational identity of the homosexual, we note a relationship based on studies which indicate that the higher the status of an occupation, the less important is sexual identity as a criterion for evaluating status and work performance. In a word, individuals in high-status positions enjoy a greater degree of tolerance for nonheterosexual activity by colleagues, clientele, and society than individuals in lower social ranks, where nonheterosexual identity becomes more salient and results in less tolerance and greater stigmatization.

This suggests the hypothesis that the salience of nonheterosexual personal identity by occupation is inversely related to occupational prestige. Although some studies have shown varying amounts of sensitivity to homosexual identities in certain occupational categories, the hypothesis in general has not yet been adequately studied. Research does indicate that a dissonant relationship exists among these identities; however, the amount of differentiation between occupational groups does not appear to vary in consistent direction (Humphreys 1972; Harry and DeVall 1978; Petras 1978; Ponse 1978; Levine 1979).

Figure 3.1 depicts an ambiguous relationship between the two group identities. Although few empirical data are available, dissonance is hypothesized on the basis of two findings:

1. One of the functions of group support for the homosexual is aristocratization, which includes challenging the heterosexual order.
2. The work environment is just one of many settings in which the heterosexual assumption is embedded (Ponse 1978).

It follows, therefore, that group homophile identity would be in conflict with occupational group identity for the majority of the nonheterosexual population. On the other hand, consonance may exist in occupations in which the heterosexual imperative is not salient.

The final category of identity, social identity *(S)*, refers to the composite of characteristics used for broad categories of identification (McCall and Simmons 1978). This process of identification is derived from what one projects, sees imaged, or has accepted by others in and from the social context (Kuhn and McPartland 1954; Klapp 1969; see Ponse 1978; Stryker 1980). Goffman (1959) views social identity as the product of the performance – the socially accepted, validated expression of self. One's social identity may be derived from only a few personal identities, or may represent a synthesis of a multiplicity of personal and group identities and positions in the social structure. It becomes a composite representation of the self perceived by others and based on observed, anticipated, and suspected behaviors, roles, or personal/group identities. In other words, social identity is defined or determined using all the information available – physiological, biological, communicative, and structural – that can be interpreted and evaluated to answer the public question, "Who are you?"

Figure 3.1, in addition, shows the differentiation between the homophile groups and accepted social identities, primarily due to the widespread acceptance of the heterosexual norm in American culture. Because homosexuality is stigmatized, homophile group activities in contemporary society are viewed as disruptive and dysfunctional to the social order. Many overt activities of homophile groups have been met with strong resistance, leading to a backlash of negativity for the identities of the participants (Harry and DeVall 1978; Ponse 1978; Levine 1979). Not only may participants fail in their attempts to integrate sexual, sex, and gender identities in the social category, they may disrupt any internal consonance among personal, group, and social identities that they enjoyed up to that time. These repercussions highlight the dissonant relationship between homophile group and social identities.

The homosexual dilemma: self-realization versus social realization

We stated above that the strong unifying character of sexuality makes it an important source of integrative symbolism on all identity levels. What happens, however, if sexuality is no longer a source of integration, and if there is differentiation among personal, group, and social categories? Part of the answer lies in the homosexual experience, rooted in the dialectical relationships of self-at-home versus self-at-work, public versus private roles, public versus private time, sexual identity and gender identity, and the primacy of sexual identity within the occupational structure.

Another part of the answer to what happens when sexuality is no longer a source of integration can be found in analyzing the choices people make throughout their lives. For the homosexual, certain choices take on an added significance, such as the decision to disclose personal sexual identity to others by joining homophile organizations and taking part in their activities, or to choose occupations that are more or less sensitive to the presence of known homosexual identities.

The motivation for "coming out" can be examined within another dialectical context: the choice between self-realization and social realization. *Self-realization* refers to "an emphasis on the integration of self with a corresponding reduction of emphasis on the integration of groups or society" (Mol 1976:145). The process of self-realization implies that individuals attempt to achieve consonance among their various identities. The object of attention is the integrated self, at the expense of increased potential dissonance among other group or social identities (cf. Turner 1976).

For the homosexual in America, emphasis on self-realization virtually guarantees social estrangement. In other words, the homosexual becomes differentiated from society because she or he contradicts the taken-for-granted heterosexual assumption. This leads to a form of identity crisis, or identity nonintegration. To freely express a nonheterosexual identity generates alienation from those adhering to the heterosexual assumption. In this respect, homophile group membership and participation indicate a concern for self-realization at the cost of social estrangement.

The other side of the relationship is an emphasis on *social realization,* defined as the integration of social and selected group identities, with a corresponding weakening of the integration of personal and other group identities. For the homosexual, the desire for social acceptance results in a resort to the secretive practices and passing strategies already described. At the same time, an emphasis on social realization has the potential for creating self-estrangement, or lack of integration of personal sexual identity with other identities. Overt compliance with the heterosexual assumption by playing it straight leads to identity crisis at the personal level, because the homosexual feels compelled to hide his or her sexual identity, thus preventing self-integration. This process results in self-estrangement, preventing integration of the core self, the repertoire of identities.

For the homosexual, this dialectic usually involves mutual exclusivity such that an emphasis on one form of fulfillment implies the impossibility of the other in pure form. An important consideration is the definition of social. In this analysis, use of the term *social* encompasses the criterion of public respectability. Although in the generic sense of the term the homosexual would be forced to choose between identity conflict or congruence at each point in the decision-making process, it would be possible to have other forms of realization or estrangement, with their concomitant forms of identity crisis (Erikson 1968:16ff). A self-realizing homosexual, for example, might also become socially realized if she or he were to gain public respectability within a community or region dominated by other homosexuals or tolerant heterosexuals. This helps to explain the gathering of homosexuals in regions such as San Francisco, where mutual support and acceptance are available.

The choices point to the emphasis on the integration effort. The dialectic generates a typology of the relationship in the ideal-typical sense, as shown in the following identity matrix:

Condition A: Self-realization and social estrangement
Condition B: Self-estrangement and social realization
Condition C: Self-realization and social realization
Condition D: Self-estrangement and social estrangement

At the center of this matrix is the impact of reference group identities (see Schmitt 1972). Groups serve an important function as mediators between personal and social identities. If the object of identity expression is self-realization, then group affiliation will be indicative of consonance among identities. For example, the homosexual who becomes a member of a homophile organization is assumed to be in search of self-integration by accepting that group identity. Those who choose not to align with, or actively participate in, homophile groups may be viewed as seeking social realization, or survival in a straight world. This hypothesis is readily testable through the empirically validated intentions of homosexuals who are members of homophile organizations, and it is consistent with imputed assumptions about those who have not chosen that overt identity, but who attempt to pass and maintain secret homosexual identities.

The influence of occupational identity on patterns of self- and social-realization has not received comparable attention. For example, one could hypothesize that homosexuals in search of self-realization would not only become members of homophile organizations, but also seek occupations that are most ambivalent toward, tolerant of, or compatible with nonheterosexual identity. Conversely, those seeking social realization would be drawn to occupations that facilitate passing practices, are more entrenched in the heterosexual assumption, and present clear boundaries between public and private roles. At the same time, the homosexual who attempts to pass would try to avoid occupations associated with persons of known homosexual identities. In the event a homosexual was forced

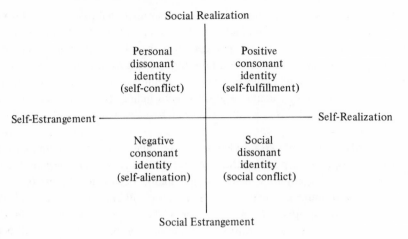

Figure 3.2 Realization and estrangement matrix.

into an occupation as the result of social class boundaries, then she or he would be expected to choose strategies that would accommodate the expression or suppression of his or her personal sexual identity.

The operationalization of the conceptual framework of identity and the relationships among personal sexual identity, homophile group affiliation, and occupational role are presented in Figure 3.2. The vertical axis represents the polar extremes of social realization and social estrangement, while the horizontal axis represents self-realization and self-estrangement. The extent to which an individual is self-realized and socially realized is indicative of a positive consonant synthesis of identities among the various categories. One who is forced, or freely chooses, to be both self-estranged and socially estranged also experiences consonance among identities; however, that consonance is negative, the ultimate in identity alienation – for example, a covert homosexual who attempts to pass, but is discovered and blackmailed (cf. Hepworth 1975).

The other two cells represent types of dissonance. One who is seeking self-realization while becoming socially estranged is representative of a socially dissonant or personally consonant identity; the individual who is socially realized but self-estranged achieves a personally dissonant or socially consonant identity. The different types of realization and estrangement can be measured through empirical indices of behavior and attitudes. We will finish our discussion by developing middle-range propositions and testable hypotheses from the incipient identity theory applied to homosexuality and occupation.

To begin with, it is possible to develop continua within the categories of personal identity, homophile group identity, and occupational role. Personal sexual identity can be measured by looking at the age at which self-labeling as a non-heterosexual was made; the self-perception of sexual identity, which can range from exclusively homosexual to exclusively heterosexual; or the expressed concern over discovery of homosexuality by significant others. Satisfaction with personal sexual identity could be grasped with indices of self-concept, ranging from positive to negative, as well as through scales that measure overall life satisfaction.

Similarly, homophile group identity can be quantified on a continuum from active participation to passive affiliation or rejection for each homophile organization, as well as length of membership. Finally, occupational identity can be measured with indices of tolerance or sensitivity within each occupational category, coupled with data on knowledge about homosexual identity on the job, number of years engaged in various occupations, problems encountered in the course of certain occupations followed by significant occupational shifts, and indices of job satisfaction compared to whether homosexuality can be expressed on the job, or whether a particular job or occupation increases or decreases homosexual activity. Scales could be constructed to measure each of these variables, making it possible to profile respondents to determine the emphasis on and extent to which there is self- or social-realization.

Toward a middle-range theory of homosexuality and occupation

We can now formulate several propositions of identity theory applied to self- and social realization and estrangement. The central propositions are as follow:

1. *The greater the emphasis on both social realization and self-realization, the more positively consonant the identity of the respondent.*
2. *The greater the emphasis on self-realization with indications of social estrangement, the more socially dissonant the identity of the respondent.*
3. *The greater the emphasis on social realization with indications of self-estrangement, the more personally dissonant the identity of the respondent.*
4. *The greater the indication of self-estrangement and social estrangement, the more negatively consonant the identity of the respondent.*

These propositions embody the network of interrelationships among self and social identities. The application of the theory to the dilemma of homosexual males in employment can be accomplished through the explication of indicators for each of the four operational variables: self-realization, self-estrangement, social realization, and social estrangement.

Once scores for self and social dimensions are calculated, we can determine the outcome of the identity-integration effort. We have further defined those possible outcomes as

1. Self-fulfillment, in which an individual is self-realized and socially realized
2. Social conflict, in which the positive effort for self-realization is accompanied by higher levels of social estrangement
3. Self-alienation, when the individual experiences high proportions of both self- and social estrangement
4. Self-conflict, where the search for social realization incidentally creates conflict through self-estrangement among personal and selected group identities

Research hypotheses

From the above, we generate testable hypotheses concerning patterns of self-realization and/or social realization, as indicated by commitment to personal sexual identity, involvement in homophile organizations, and occupation of respondent.

Hypothesis 1a: *The greater the focus on self-realization, the more active the respondent in homophile organizations.*

Hypothesis 1b: *The greater the focus on self-realization, the more active the respondent in homophile organizations that are politically involved in change.*

The underlying rationale for these hypotheses is that homophile organizations serve as a means of reinforcing personal sexual identity. The more actively the individual is involved in an organization, and the longer the association, the greater is the motivation toward self-realization as a homosexual. At the same time, the type of participation within the organization is considered to be significant, so that holding major offices or serving on committees points to more overt behavior as a homosexual, contrasted with more secretive practices. Hypothesis 1b reflects the expectation that involvement in homophile organizations that are politically oriented in their activities indicates greater emphasis on the part of the respondent to bringing about social change in order to make it possible for homosexuals to experience self-realization among all categories of identity.

Hypothesis 2a: *The salience of homosexual personal identity on the job is inversely related to occupational prestige.*

Hypothesis 2b: *The greater the perceived separation between public and private roles, the greater the perception that problems with co-workers and employers are the result of homosexual identity.*

Hypothesis 2c: *The greater the perception that homosexual identity adversely affects occupation, the lower the participation in homophile organizations and the greater the concern with being discovered.*

These hypotheses investigate the interrelationships among personal sexual identity, homophile group identity, and occupational identity. Perception has important consequences in this section, especially in terms of how the respondent views the impact of involvement in one area on another. In determining occupational prestige, objective criteria can be used, based on standard scales and indices of occupations (Blau and Duncan 1967).

Hypothesis 3a: *The younger the respondent, the greater the expressed job dissatisfaction.*
Hypothesis 3b: *The greater the emphasis on self-realization and the lower the prestige of the occupation, the greater the job instability.*
Hypothesis 3c: *The older the respondent, the greater the belief that knowledge of homosexuality would cause problems at work.*

These hypotheses explore the impact homosexual identity has on occupations and career patterns. The work histories and levels of job satisfaction are relatively stable for male homosexuals, contradicting the general assumption that the majority of male homosexuals experience high job instability, even when homosexuality becomes known or suspected. Bell and Weinberg (1978) found that homosexual males did not tend to shift from job to job when their sexual orientation became known or suspected. Nor were they forced to stay in unpleasant or unsatisfying positions, as indicated by the high levels of job satisfaction expressed by young and old respondents. Considering that the data on which those findings were based were collected in the late 1960s and early 1970s, a current study could determine if the conclusions are still valid. In addition, certain hypotheses explore relationships that have not been previously investigated, such as the impact of age on levels of job satisfaction, and perceptions about the impact that knowledge of their homosexuality would have for respondents.

Hypothesis 4a: *The younger the respondent, the more importance placed on the perceived acceptance of homosexuality within an occupation in making a career choice, and the more occupational choice is based on self-identification as a homosexual.*
Hypothesis 4b: *The greater the emphasis on self-realization, the greater the extent to which occupational choice is influenced by the job location in a gay community or servicing of a gay clientele.*

These hypotheses look specifically at the relationship between occupational choice and sexual identity. Again, Bell and Weinberg (1978) found that many of their respondents felt being gay had not particularly affected their careers, although a few indicated that their homosexuality had restricted job opportunities. On the other hand, some reported that being homosexual was advantageous to them. Harry and DeVall (1978) conclude that homosexual self-identification appears to have significant impact on occupational choice, as evidenced by the grouped distribution of gay males within the occupational structure. Their study did not, however, look at the importance placed on complementarity between sexual identity and career choice.

These are but a few of the many hypotheses that can be generated to look at the relationships among sexual identity, occupational identity, and homophile involvement (see J. Teitge 1981). An empirical investigation that tests these hypotheses can support the general theoretical assumption which underlies the research design: Two of the most important identities for an individual are gender identity, as complemented or contradicted by personal sexual identity, and occupational identity. The research design illustrates that it is possible to operationalize conditions of identity consonance or dissonance. Our present aim is merely to exemplify that operationalization by using gender, homosexual, and occupational identities, highlighting their respective interrelationships and consequences for the integration effort.

Summary

In this chapter, the framework of identity theory was elaborated and applied to the relationships among self, identity, and role. Particular emphasis was placed on the definition and parameters of the body's identity as a ''sex.'' Gender identity and sexual identity have been selected as the primary objects of analysis, with transsexualism and homosexuality serving to exemplify how identities interrelate. At the same time, a middle-range theory of homosexuality and occupation was presented from a conceptual model of identity categories, and a number of hypotheses generated concerning the relationships among sexual identity, occupational identity, homophile group identity, and other identity categories. Paradoxes of gender identity were noted, and implications of these ironies for identity maintenance at the interactional level and change at the institutional or societal level suggested. Finally, the issues were formulated into propositions and reflected in the research design for future study of identity integration.

4. Extending identity theory beyond bodies:
prenatal and postmortem identities

This chapter attempts crucial illustrations of identity as a social construction. In the first part, the concept of prenatal identity (PNI) is briefly described as a speculative notion that is real despite the absence of a separately embodied individual. Before an individual is born, most of his or her ascribed identities have already been established by family, friends, and society. Consequently, a baby enters the world with a predetermined identity repertoire, the self typified in infancy, merely waiting for a body through which it can be physically manifested.

While family, friends, and professionals await the arrival of the new social actor, others set about the task of constructing an identity for the invisible, socially unembodied fetus toward which their behavior is directed. We begin our discussion by introducing the notion of identities without bodies as a fundamental problematic in the sociological psychology literature. Secondly, PNI is described as a necessary preconstruction project by which the fetal object is endowed with meaning and potential selfhood. The process of preconstruction is exemplified by the social construction of a pregnancy identity, by the extension of medical technology to define conditions and characteristics of the fetus, and by the similarities between mourning for perinatal deaths and other grief adjustment processes. Finally, we briefly describe birth as a social event in which PNI is further objectivated through embodiment in situations and through formal introduction into the preexistent social structure. The second section of the chapter explores the existence, dimensions, and impact of postmortem identity (PMI) on contemporary conceptualizations of self-maintenance and biographical reconstruction. The main line of argumentation is that one's identity is a vehicle for self-presentation and synthesis over the life course (Schutz 1962); transcends the biologic entity; and becomes symbolically meaningful as a social essence even after the organism ceases to exist (Katz 1975). In other words, identities of the deceased continue to play a significant role in the social interactions of those who have validated and objectified those identities.

92

The second section is directed toward the development of a theoretical framework by which PMI can be defined and measured as a sociological psychology construct. First, we present a review of current perspectives on death and dying, and explore the denial of death as the predominant cultural stance in America. Next, we describe the relationship between death and identity, with specific emphasis on the search for symbolic immortality. Death identity is introduced as the construct by which survivors redefine the cadaver as a meaningful entity.

The theoretical orientation to identity as a social construction is illustrated by the development of a conceptual model of PMI. We suggest that PMI as an interpersonal reconstruction project is an underdeveloped area for empirical sociological psychology. As a first step to fill the gap, we report the preliminary findings of a pilot study into the existence, dimensions, and impact of PMI on contemporary efforts at self-maintenance and biographical reconstruction. The conclusion from this theoretical and empirical treatment of embodiment and identity is that PNI and PMI are useful technical tools for further understanding social attitudes toward, and perceptions about, persons as objectified in American society.

Prenatal identity: life before birth

Prenatal identity (PNI) refers to self's identity before the biological organism is born. The concept is intended to account for the initial prepartum identity for a fetus that is as much a part of the life course of that individual as any other identity he or she seeks or has bestowed between birth and death. The literature in sociological psychology is replete with theoretical essays and empirical studies of identities constructed throughout the life course. Most of the research focuses on identities tied to bodies. An underlying assumption is that the two, identities and bodies, are inexorably tied; and this is the basic premise underlying the use of "co-presence" and "appresentation" in studies of interaction, such as Goffman's (1963) disciplined inquiry into face-to-face encounters and stigmatization, and his formulation of the dramaturgical approach to symbolic interactionism. As we also noted earlier, a fundamental source of identity is embodiment in situations, or the implication that interaction is mutual physical appresentation.

A second major assumption of sociological psychologists is that individuals are both determiners of and determined by their social environment, or producers and products of society. Consequently, it is difficult to conceive of identities that have not been *mutually* negotiated between parties to an interaction. Yet we also acknowledge the process of identity "bestowal," through which identities are imposed on individuals whether or not they seek such labeling or classification. The concept of PNI exemplifies this structural imposition. We begin by discussing the notion of identities without bodies as basic to the conceptualization of PNI. We end by looking at birth as a social event through which PNI becomes sociohistorically available and empirically validated through "delivery" of the biological organism into the existing social structure.

Identities without bodies

The concept of identity is fruitfully extended by Maines (1978) in his discussion of the dilemma faced by demographers of conceptualizing bodies and selves. He begins with an analytic, and to some extent substantive, distinction between bodies, or the physical aspect of human existence, and identities, or the social categories into which people are placed and given meaning (see Mead's biologic individual vs. self, 1934). He argues that demographers traditionally discuss *bodies* rather than *identities,* thereby ignoring that which is particularly social about human beings. Of course, Maines admits there is a methodological rationale for counting only the physical dimension, since bodies are much easier to tabulate. Unlike identities, bodies can be in only one place at one time, and only one body can occupy a given space. Yet, as McCall and Simmons (1978) note, it is identities that mobilize social interaction.

To illustrate this point, Maines cites the example of a first child for a married couple. While demographers add one person to the population, multiple identities are constructed, such as father, mother, son or daughter, grandparent. One new body gives rise to many new identities. He states: "It is true that these family identities exist as consensual objects *prior* to birth, and in that sense are merely appropriated . . ." (1978:243, italics added). Even before birth, before the child's body becomes an object added to the population, the anticipated self is objectivated for family and significant others.

This dialectic of bodies and identities illustrates the transcendent nature of self. We argue that identities are socially real and objectified without physical embodiment; and that we orient our behavior toward them just as meaningfully as we do to other identities that are physically presented to us. The concept of PNI exemplifies this purposeful orientation of behavior to unembodied but real "social things."

PNI as a preconstruction project

We recall from Chapter 2 that society preexists the individual in every way. When individuals are born, they immediately become situated in a network of social relations and social structures. Through no effort on his or her part, the newborn child is given a name, a gender, an ethnic heritage, a socioeconomic status, a family of orientation, a birth order, an age, an attractiveness category, a health condition, and any number of other "classifications" that transform the neonate into a social actor. PNI, however, is not directly concerned with these so-called infant identities. We take the analysis back one step to identities before birth that allow us to act meaningfully toward the unborn child. Three areas illustrate PNI as a preconstruction project:

1. The indirect link through what has been termed the "pregnant" identity
2. Enabling medical technology that demystifies fetal development and thereby imaginatively "embodies" the potential social actor
3. The impact of perinatal death, for which survivors often mourn as though they knew the unborn "person"

1. PNI through the pregnant identity: We are indebted to Miller (1978) for her research into the social construction of physiological events, particularly identity in pregnancy. Complementing our sociological psychological perspective, Miller notes at the outset that her study "was designed to examine the basic Meadian/Schutzian assertions that all identities are acquired through processes of social construction of reality which may be independent of 'objective' reality. . . . Within this framework, this paper focuses upon the *social construction and reconstruction of pregnancy*" (1978: 181–2, her italics). In other words, she views social and physiological pregnancy as "separate phenomena which are only brought together by elaborate social effort that (1) creates the meaning of pregnancy as the appropriate signs appear, or (2) re-creates it as the perspective is acquired that allows for reassessment" (p. 182).

Although organic pregnancy is a physiological fact, it is an objective condition that nonetheless has social meaning only to the extent that meaning is attached to it through interactional processes. These processes include objectification through identity bestowal by others, such as family, friends, professionals; subjectification through internal conversations between the I and the Me about the growing fetus; or intersubjectification through interaction with others who have taken on or can interpret the pregnancy identity.

PNI also denotes a dialectic between physiological and social phenomena to the extent that prenatal identity construction is dependent upon the objectification of the biological organism as a "thing" toward which action is oriented. As a particular social construction, PNI must be based on a physiological and/or social pregnancy identity, and the dimensions or boundaries of PNI are dependent upon the identities produced by the presence or absence of physiological and/or social pregnancy. To illustrate, we elaborate on Miller's identity matrix (1978: 182) to include the presence or absence of PNI in the four identities she described, each under two conditions: (1) when the woman believes she is pregnant (self-defined

Physiologically Pregnant

	Yes	No
Yes (Socially Pregnant)	"Normal" pregnancy Established PNI that is biologically, psychologically, and socially stable	"False" social and psychological pregnancy Nonembodied social and psychological PNI
No (Socially Pregnant)	Socially undiscovered pregnancy (real secret) No social PNI; psychological PNI and biological embodiment	Nonpregnancy (unreal secret) No social PNI; no biological embodiment; only psychological PNI

(a)

Physiologically Pregnant

	Yes	No
Yes (Socially Pregnant)	Closed awareness pregnancy (woman not told or cognizant) Social PNI and embodiment that is psychologically dissonant	False social pregnancy Nonembodied social PNI
No (Socially Pregnant)	Undiscovered pregnancy No PNI; only biological embodiment	Nonpregnancy No PNI

(b)

Figure 4.1   Prenatal identity (PNI) linked to pregnancy identity: (a) Woman believes she is pregnant (psychologically pregnant); (b) woman does not believe she is pregnant (not psychologically pregnant). *Part (a) adapted from Miller (1978).*

or psychologically pregnant); and (2) when the woman does not believe she is pregnant (not psychologically pregnant). Figures 4.1a and 4.1b combine the physiological, psychological, and social levels of analysis and apply them to the "fact of pregnancy."

As we see in Figure 4.1a, if a woman believes she is pregnant, there can be a PNI with or without the physical reality of a fetus, as long as physiological changes are attributed to a pregnant condition or there is self-definition as one who is pregnant. There can also be a psychologically real PNI and a biologically viable fetus with no social PNI if the physiological signs are not attributed to a condition of pregnancy by others, or no pregnancy identity is bestowed. In Figure 4.1b, we note that when the woman does not believe she is pregnant, there can be a social PNI that creates psychological dissonance. Very young and pregnant girls may have to be informed by parents or school officials about the meaning of their "swelling." The validation of a pregnant identity through physiological cues and social definition results in a condition of closed awareness if the woman is not told or does not understand about her pregnancy. In terms of the other conditions of physiological and social pregnancy, the absence of self-definition does not affect the construction or absence of PNI. In the event the woman does not believe she is pregnant and there is no social PNI, yet a biological organism exists, the birthing process eventually triggers the construction of an infant identity even though no meaningful PNI was involved.

Another instructive aspect of Miller's work is the interrelationships among the constructed identities of pregnant woman/mother, expectant father, and the PNI imputed to the fetal self. Once a pregnancy is constructed or reconstructed, the project of constructing PNI begins. The extent to which PNI is defined depends largely upon the planning of and reaction to the pregnancy identity. Miller speaks of three categories of planners: (1) the true planner who becomes pregnant intentionally, (2) the "sort-of" planner who "happens" into pregnancy, and (3) the nonplanner who does not intend to get pregnant. We hypothesize that, for the true planners, PNI construction begins in a woman's fantasy life and conversations prior to conception, and no later than recognition of symptoms that lead to the self-definition as pregnant. In this instance, social and psychological PNI could exist prior to biological PNI.

For the sort-of planner, the construction of PNI probably begins when physiological pregnancy has been confirmed and a social pregnancy identity has been successfully negotiated. Finally, for the group of nonplanners, social and psychological PNI may not be constructed until very late in the pregnancy, if at all, since based on Miller's findings neither the physiological or the social pregnancy identity is readily accepted or negotiated by this group. This last pattern could be studied among unforeseen teenage pregnancies.

Other empirical patterns apply to those women who become temporarily pregnant physically and psychologically, only to terminate in natural and scarcely noticed abortions. For those who become physiologically pregnant and seek surgical abortions, however, the links between social and psychological identity bestowal may be decisive: to keep the pregnancy a total secret, or to bestow a negative identity on the fetus, such as intruder or obstacle to career, life-style, or marriage. The PNI of pregnant women seeking abortions versus those coerced into abortions versus those choosing to bear the child would differ in patterns of motivation and in linkages to social structure. The link between PNI and pregnancy identity, however, does not directly address the issue of *what* constitutes a prenatal identity. For that, we turn our attention to the impact of enabling technology on PNI.

2. *PNI as a technological by-product:* When the construction of a prenatal identity begins, there are general categories into which the fetal self can be placed. Available information allows us to narrow the range of possible identities the fetal self may possess. For example, commonsense knowledge tells us that the fetus is human, biologically male or female, and a member of a racial/ethnic group. Beyond these categories, our ability to predict certain physical characteristics loses its precision. Such features as hair or eye color, skin tone, height, beauty, weight, IQ, and general health are often talked about in folk categories based on lore or myth. We can only guess at the age of the fetus, based on empirically constructed measures using the cessation of menstruation, fetal heart rate or movement, and weight gain of the mother as guidelines. For the most part, construction of PNI is an exercise in probability and "guesstimation" for ity of pregnant mothers, expectant fathers, and even medical professionals.

Contemporary society, with its scientific and technological knowledge base, has new tactics for predicting characteristics of PNI. As a result of our rational preoccupation with enhancing the quality of life, we can now demystify fetal development in order to monitor the physical and mental condition of the human presocial actor. Genetic counseling enables couples to assess the probabilities of certain types of offspring resulting from their pregnancy decisions. Such techniques as ultrasound, or sonograms, enable us to "see" the fetus by means of sound waves bounced around inside the uterus. The resulting data assist the physician in estimating the viability and maturity of the fetus. Another technique, amniocentesis, enables us to investigate chromosomal irregularities and describe the physiological condition of the fetus.

While these and similar techniques may have been intended to assess the viability of the fetus or uncover abnormal aspects of pregnancy, they have served also to enhance our powers for constructing prenatal identity. We can learn the sex of a fetus, discover physical deformities, or be warned about potential mental handicaps. Technology can eliminate some of the guesswork surrounding the organic characteristics of a fetus. Identities bestowed as a result of these technological transformations may indeed be fateful for the fetus: A negative PNI may lead to a decision to abort.

Similarly, the use of intrauterine photography has not only demystified the process of fetal development, but also allowed us to visually "embody" an otherwise invisible, socially unembodied self. Because embodiment is a fundamental source of identity, the availability of intrauterine photography permits us to extend the process of identity construction to prebirth situations. Through advances in genetic engineering, the occasional success of test-tube fertilization, the rise of artificial insemination and surrogate mothering, and the availability of Nobel Prize sperm banks, the potential exists for the planned construction of PNI prior to conception.

Examination of those issues, however, is beyond the scope of this chapter. Let us merely state that a more elaborate PNI is a by-product of medical technology which now gives us access to information as the basis for identities of the fetal self previously unavailable until the imposition of postpartum infant identities. Finally, we turn our attention to a third area that illustrates the social construction of PNI: perinatal death.

3. Perinatal death and mourning: post-factum evidence of PNI: We realize that if identity as a concept is elusive, then PNI as a speculative construct is even more difficult to pin down. To illustrate our thesis that PNI is an objectivated, constructed identity toward which actions are oriented, we engage in a mild phenomenological reduction of perinatal death. In particular, we are concerned with the phenomenon of mourning for the unborn social actor as indicative of the existence of PNI.

In their book *Motherhood and Mourning* (1980), Peppers and Knapp discuss several characteristics common to grieving mothers whether their experience involves fetal or infant death. For example, they hypothesize that a mother would be more emotionally distant from the child if she miscarried at six months than if she lost a baby who had lived several hours or days. In other words, they "expected that grief expression would be less intense in cases of miscarriage than in stillbirth or neonatal death" (1980:19). What they found through interviews, however, was that "the duration of grieving was generally shorter in the case of fetal loss, but the initial expression of grief was just as intense" (1980:19). Another similarity concerns the mother's memory of vivid details surrounding the loss, regardless of whether the loss was through miscarriage, stillbirth, or neonatal death. "Each mother was able to recall the specific circumstances of her pregnancy and loss. . . . This acute remembrance was one thing that every mother, without exception, had in common" (1980:20).

What emerges from these similarities is that perinatal death, including the death of a fetus, is perceived as a loss that is not only physiologically real, but that can have a profound effect on the social, emotional, and physical well-being of the mother. As Peppers and Knapp (1980:15) observed: "A period of grief and mourning, doubts and fears, questions with no answers, and intense sadness often follows fetal death." These emotions of confusion, resentment, and guilt differ little from the stages of grief experienced by the loss of adults with established identities (Kavanaugh 1972; Kubler-Ross 1975).

For many friends and professionals, the period of maternal grief following fetal death is one they can neither understand nor fully comprehend. For the mother, and perhaps the father and other immediate family members, the loss is real and significant. The sense of loss must focus on an object, and that object is the prenatal identity bestowed on the fetal self. In particular, fetal movement or "quickening" leads to the perception of the fetus as a separate, identified individual:

From quickening until birth the mother busies herself with preparations for the new arrival – establishing a nursery, buying clothes, attending baby showers. She also uses quiet moments of reflection to fantasize about the baby, its sex, its appearance, its personality. She begins to give the baby an *identity* and a name. She may even talk to it or indirectly touch it by caressing her abdomen. (Peppers and Knapp 1980:61, italics added)

The objectification of a biological fetus into a self toward which meaningful behavior is oriented is the construction of PNI.

In conclusion, we find that research into the phenomenon of mourning in situations of perinatal death helps us to conceptualize the notion of PNI and to grasp its meaning as an identity imputed to a socially nonembodied self. On the other hand, PNI serves as a useful technical term for understanding the significance of mourning and grief for mothers and immediate others. Therefore, once we recognize that PNI exists as a real, objectivated dimension of the fetus-soon-to-be-social-actor, we can both appreciate the grieving process in the event of fetal loss and direct our energies toward helping family, friends, and professionals to grasp the significance of the loss in their interaction with the bereaved.

Birth as a social event

Once construction of PNI has begun, its dimensions are shaped and reshaped as new information becomes available and birth approaches. As we noted above, technological developments have made it possible to define the PNI of a fetus so that most of the general characteristics, such as sex, stage of development, normality, and physical condition, can be confirmed. Yet it is not until the moment of birth, the time of delivery into the social world, that the physiological and social components of the objectivated fetal self converge and are fused into an infant identity. Birth, therefore, is a social event by which the fetal self is transformed into a sociohistorically validated actor. This emerging self is immediately situated in interactional contexts and simultaneously actualizes an array of identities: gender, religious, social age, socioeconomic, and so on. Components of the prenatal identity, such as biological sex, are confirmed and constructed into gender and associated identities. From the moment of birth, the individual will

spend the course of his or her life presenting, negotiating, and validating a multiplicity of identities initially imposed by others.

This is not to say that PNI disappears at the moment of birth. Because it has
not been internalized, PNI does not directly become part of the neonate's own
repertoire of identities. For those who engage in the construction and bestowal
of PNI, however, particularly the mother who can recall interacting with the
fetus, it is an identity that remains an object in memory, and interaction with the
neonate may continue to be affected by that identity. Mothers may modify later
identities by conflating them with PNI, as in the case of a favorite son who had
an easy gestation or another not so appreciated during whose term the mother
suffered greatly. As we saw in the case of perinatal death, mothers were able to
recall seemingly obscure details of their pregnancies – of their infant's PNI.
Such memory, once constructed, does not totally disappear as it enters into the
construction of later identities by those responsible for the child's socialization.
We turn our attention now to another speculative concept indirectly linked to the
same issues underlying PNI: postmortem identity, the identity that lingers after
death, just as PNI awaited us before birth.

Postmortem identity: life after death

Within the framework of identities without bodies *before* independent physical
existence, we can consider an identity that is socially constructed *after* the individual ceases to be a biologically living member of the community. The idea of
postmortem identity (PMI), or identity after death, is meaningful to sociological
psychologists because it helps to account for the full range of identities that are
socially constructed before, during, and after our physical lifetimes. Although
some studies have hinted at the presence of social life after bodily death, researchers to date have not developed an analytical tool. The following sections
attempt to fill the gap by unpacking the concept of postmortem identity within
our theoretical perspective.

Death and dying: a review

Death and dying have long been frequent topics in anthropology, medicine, psychiatry, psychology, and religion. Until the late 1950s, however, the study of
death and dying was virtually ignored by sociologists (Faunce and Fulton 1958).
The edited volume by Feifel (1959), *The Meaning of Death,* indicated that the
sociological literature on death and dying was growing.

Recent sociological studies can be divided into four categories, based on the
focus of their research efforts. The first group investigates the process of dying

as a social phenomenon. It looks at the social and psychological problems associated with dying assessed from the viewpoint of the dying person, family, friends, medical practitioners, and others (Fox 1959; Glaser and Strauss 1964; Brim 1970). The second group of studies focuses on the functionaries of death, such as physicians, nurses, morgue attendants, clergy, and funeral directors. The researchers examine such issues as the role of funeral directors, public attitudes toward funerals and funeral directors, and the role conflict between funeral directors and clergy (Fulton 1961; Sudnow 1967; Pine 1975).

Effects of death are explored in the third category of research. Specific attention is paid to the impact of death on society, the cost of dying, and the administration of death (Gorer 1965; Blauner 1966; Fulton 1967; Pine and Phillips 1970; Fulton and Fulton 1971; Simmons et al. 1972). These studies are valuable because they analyze the mortuary costs and practices that reflect the organization and cultural values of society.

Finally, a fourth category of sociological literature evaluates funeral ritual and specific industry for what they claim has been the "commercialism" of the funeral ritual. In addition, they are critical of:

1. The efforts by funeral directors to disguise death through restoration and cosmetic "heroics"
2. The setting of funeral homes, which indirectly contributes to the sensationalism and cost of dying
3. The use of argot to maintain a death work mystique
4. The form of contemporary funeral practices, which exploit the survivors and bereaved (Bowman 1959; Harmer 1963; Mitford 1963; Morgan 1973).

Much research and controversy surrounding death and dying have surfaced as a result of two distinct yet overlapping events: the rationalization of the funeral industry, such as the claim for professional status by funeral directors; and renewed debate over definitions of death and strategies sought to circumvent the inevitability and finality of death (Lofland 1978). The first event, rationalization of the industry, is not directly addressed here, although the emphasis on cosmetic heroics and body restoration by funeral directors has been documented (see D. Teitge 1981). More important, we must examine definitions of death as they influence current conceptualizations of what death is and how it affects everyday life.

1. Definitions of death: Sociologists have explored the various standards by which death is defined (Sudnow 1967). In reviewing traditional criteria of death, Charmaz (1980:109) explains that life-sustaining technology makes these traditional criteria inadequate. The development and use of artificial respirators and other life-prolonging equipment underscores the issue of what constitutes death and when it occurs (Cassel 1974; Dempsey 1975; Devins and Diamond 1977).

In effect, biological death is the culmination of several stages of biological and physiological deterioration (ISELS 1977; Kastenbaum 1977; Schulz 1978). The first stage is clinical death, when spontaneous heartbeat and respiration cease. Next is brain death, indicated by the complete lack of oxygen to the brain. The third state, biological death, occurs when there is no brain activity, as typically measured by electroencephalogram monitoring. Finally, cellular death means that there is a cessation of all functioning of bodily organs and cells.

Although these stages constitute a typical progression of organic deterioration, the order through which an individual passes may vary. For example, heart and lung machines, or respirators, have altered the process in some cases so that brain death or biological death preceded clinical death. Consequently, the criteria of death have been reevaluated in order to fix the point at which death verdicts are rendered and certificates are issued to legitimate the social passage from being alive to being dead. There is a certain paradox surrounding these new criteria. The search for such criteria is both a product and a reflection of the continued dilemma of the denial of death in American society.

2. Denial of death in America: In her work on the sociology of death and bereavement, Sheskin (1979) notes there is an assumption in the literature on death and dying that beliefs in the inevitability of death are repressed and denied. American views of death are interpreted as a cultural "taboo" by researchers such as Aries (1974), Farberow (1966), Kubler-Ross (1975), Pine (1974), and Weisman (1972). In an effort to account for death-avoidance patterns in American culture, Feifel (1977:5, italics added) contends: "In a society that emphasizes achievement and the future, the prospect of no future at all and *loss of identity* is an abomination. Death is seen as destroyer of the American vision – the right to life, liberty, and the pursuit of happiness. Hence, death and dying invite our hostility and repudiation." Comparable analysis of the meaning of death in Western culture is found in the work of Becker (1975:ix), who indicated: "The idea of death, the fear of it, haunts the human animal like nothing else; it is a mainspring of human activity – activity designed largely to avoid the fatality of death. . . ." While interest in death is not a new development, the strategies employed to facilitate denial have only recently become the objects of analysis in a variety of disciplines (Schulz 1978). What is denial, and what form does it take in typical responses to death anxiety?

In researching the social reality of death, Charmaz (1980) notes that the term *denial of death* is actually used in three contexts: (1) to indicate disbelief in the death of self, (2) to describe a negation of death as a condition of human existence, and (3) to depict a cultural stance toward death. At the same time, there is a need to distinguish denial from other repression tactics, such as deception, avoidance, and concealment. Studies generally indicate a diversity of opinions over what factors clearly signify denial rather than merely representing an inability to cope with the reality of death (Gorer 1965; Kastenbaum and Aisenberg 1972; Parkes, 1972; Lofland 1978).

We believe that Becker's (1975) work, *The Denial of Death,* synthesizes the major theoretical perspectives that address the fundamental issue of denial. He views the underlying determinant of denial to be fear of death. Relying on psychoanalytic and existential interpretations, Becker posits:

1. Humans are unable to face their own death.
2. This results in a "fear" of death in general.
3. The inability to face death fears leads individuals to deny death through attempts to overcome the fears.
4. Subsequently, the fear of death itself becomes repressed, a condition that is both psychologically and socially unhealthy.

Based on the thesis that a full confrontation with death would result in psychosis, Becker contends that the symbolic construction of the human character serves intentionally to perpetuate the denial of death. Human character is therefore socially constructed, and it constitutes a "vital lie," since it refuses to confront death in a meaningful way. In other words, individuals seek to avoid despair, including that which accompanies the reality of death, by constructing a false sense of self-worth and personal power. It is paradoxical that individuals need the vital lie, the sense of worth and power, in order to live a life the end of which they deny, but cannot avoid.

The presence and influence of the denial of death in American society leads to the search for means of conquering it. Historically, religious belief in a spiritual world has countered the finality of death. Belief in the afterlife is signaled by the cemetery monuments of Western society. The increasing secularization of society, however, has fostered efforts to find other strategies to assist denial. Advances in technology have produced a new denial strategy.

3. Denial strategies: The advent of cryonics: Cryonics, the technique of suspending or freezing tissues using liquid nitrogen, originated in Europe during the 1940s (Sheskin 1979). The application of the procedure to human beings was explained by physicist Richard Ettinger in *The Prospect of Immortality* (1964). He concluded that humans could be chemically suspended and preserved with minimal cellular damage until restoration could be accomplished at some future date.

In evaluating the emergence of cryonic societies that promote and perform cryonic suspension, we see that personal or survivor-initiated suspension represents a new death-denying tactic that is technologically based and legitimated in a science-oriented society. Denial is evidenced by three analogies between Becker's thesis and the characteristics of cryonics:

1. The presence of linguistic euphemisms
2. The shift in the American stance toward death in its endorsement of cryonic technology and aristocratization of an otherwise deviant subculture
3. The quest for heroism through the transference of power to cryonicists

Furthermore, adherence to the cryonic philosophy exemplifies an additional social construct in the death-denying "vital lie" of human character.

To begin with, euphemisms employed in cryonic circles constitute a denial-of-death language. The cryonic process is called *suspension* rather than embalming, and one who is so treated is *suspended,* not dead. The individual is *stored,* rather than the body or corpse being buried or entombed. Since a casket is not functional or appropriate, storage is maintained through the use of a *Forever Flask.* The flask occupant, who is prepared by a cryonicist and not a mortician, is referred to as the *patient.* A removable top on the flask allows for *annual* viewing of the suspended patient.

Cryonic language communicates a denial of death in the very act of conversing about "suspended patients," and conversation is, par excellence, mundane reality construction (Berger and Luckmann 1966). Even though a person has been declared legally dead, relatives and friends are linguistically led into believing that the loved one is merely "on hold" until a scientific cure and reanimation is perfected. This belief is reinforced by the language of practitioners and survivors alike, which excludes any reference to death.

The rise of cryonics as a denial strategy also reflects a shift in the American stance toward death. Just as Dumont and Foss (1973) found that the magical reversal of death in literature and television represents denial for children, so the advent of cryonics, with its scientific and technological credibility, depicts the potential for holding the body in a potentially living condition and restoring it to life at a later date. In addition, science and technology are the main universes of discourse for stating what the world is really like. They constitute privileged kinds of knowledge; denial thus gains great potential mythological power now that there is a scientific version of it, along with traditional religious versions.

Finally, agreeing on suspension can be interpreted as an attempted act of heroism. Becker (1975) contends that, regardless of how one attempts to realize it, heroism is central to human existence. Humans demonstrate an innate need for heroism that, although it may be unconscious, is acted upon nonetheless. Use of cryonic techniques is viewed as an heroic endeavor in two ways. First, the possibility of being the first suspended patient to be successfully revived denotes heroic anticipation. Simply making a contribution to research by serving in an experiment exemplifies an act of heroism to some extent. Secondly, Becker's notion of transference is applicable. He defines transference as the projection of magical power on a leader with whom the individual identifies and on whom he or she is dependent. Whether transference is made by the patient or by survivors, the cryonicist becomes the leader who controls the fate of the suspended. Consequently, the cryonicist is given a heroic role that is vicariously shared by the individual patients.

The discussion of PMI serves to underscore the extent to which individuals attempt to deny the reality of death. Technological developments and an extraordinary scientific optimism have stimulated an interest in cryonics as a viable strategy for eluding the inevitable. Yet the discussion also brings a more fundamental issue into focus: the overwhelming desire to cling tenaciously to one's identity across time and space. We recall a basic theme from Feifel's (1977:5) discussion of death as a cultural taboo: "The prospect of no future at all and *loss of identity* is an abomination" (emphasis added). To accept the prospect that one's self may be no more than a forgettable and degradable historical artifact is to mock human yearning. Humans fear death not only as an end of physical life, but also as an end of social existence. To investigate death without considering its relationship to identity would only gloss the deep structure of meaning.

Death and identity

As Fulton (1965:3) so simply states: "Death asks us for our identity. Confronted by death, man is compelled to provide in some form a response to the question: Who am I?" Perhaps more specifically, we contend that when confronted with death, one is compelled to consider the issue of how he or she wants to be remembered. Such a question points to a fundamental proposition presented in previous chapters: Identities are socially constructed through mutual validation between social actors and their audiences. Coming face to face with the reality of death, or pondering the limits of biological existence, brings the finality of death into sharp focus. We feel that, under these circumstances, individuals are provided one last chance to shape their identities, rank them, and assist in the final synthesis of the individual self. Two aspects of death and identity are explored below: (1) symbolic immortality as a means of validating physical and social existence, and (2) the concept and effects of a death-identity as the final definition of the self.

1. Symbolic immortality: In his books *Life of the Self* and *The Broken Connection,* Lifton (1976, 1979) discusses his theory of symbolic immortality. He argues that death and the continuity of life are basic to an understanding of human existence and have become problematic in our historical context. Briefly stated, his formative–symbolic perspective posits that the process of symbolization is an integral characteristic of the psychic condition. In facing death, Lifton (1976: 31) contends:

[E]ven in our unconscious lives we are by no means convinced of our own immortality. . . . We both "know" that we will die and resist and fail to act upon that knowledge. Nor is the need to transcend death *mere* denial. More essentially, it represents a compelling universal urge to maintain an inner sense of continuous symbolic relationship, over time and space. . . .

Lifton emphasizes that he is referring to a *sense* of immortality, which is neither compensatory nor pathological. Rather, it serves as one's symbolization of the ties with both biological acquaintances and history, with the past and the future. Eternal survival through symbolization points to a perceived need to change one's environmental context so that a self will be perpetuated beyond death. This is the particular and definitive *human* problematic.

To support his thesis, Lifton cites five general modes of achieving a sense of immortality:

1. The *biological* mode, or sense of living on through an endless chain of children and grandchildren
2. The *theological* mode, or belief that death is the release from a profane life to existence on a spiritual plane
3. The *creative* mode, or sense of immortality through personal achievements and contributions that endure through future generations
4. The *eternal nature* mode, or belief that immortality rests in nature itself
5. The *experiential transcendence* mode, or a psychic state of such ecstasy that any restrictions on the senses, including the sense of mortality, disappear

In his early formulation, Lifton attempted to make sense of survivors' reactions to such devastating experiences as the atomic bombing of Hiroshima. He felt that studying an extreme situation would lead to insights about routine death and ordinary people. However, it is obvious from his model that he focused on a psychologistic analysis not strongly grounded in sociological psychology. If a sociological perspective were integrated with Lifton's symbolic immortality theory, it would enhance the interpretive contribution and analytical power of his paradigm. We suggest a sixth means of achieving immortality – namely, the *ritualization mode*, or a socially constructed immortal identity that represents a combination of any or all of the other modes. While Lifton focused primarily on the psychic sense of immortality, he overlooked the cultural importance the ritualization of death has on the psychic reality of beliefs about, and a sense of, immortality. The internalization of norms and values relevant to death rituals has the same potential for accentuating a sense of immortality that it has for other psychic states.

There is little doubt that individuals do not want to be remembered as being dead; they want to be remembered as living. Just as Lifton's modes provide a sense of immortality through symbolization, the ritualization of death serves an important function by allowing survivors to undertake an inventory of the symbols and their meanings that have been purposively and carefully bequeathed to significant others and society by the deceased.

In American society, death ritualization typically takes the form of funerals and burials (Grollman 1974; Raether and Slater 1975). These rituals are viewed as necessary not only for the psychological and spiritual benefit of grief adjustment, but also as a means of putting a sense of closure on the life of one who has died (Gorer 1965, Dempsey 1975). Funerary rituals allow survivors to reintegrate the group and dispel the ambivalent attraction-horror elicited by the corpse (Malinowski 1948:47–53). The death ritual serves as a symbolic expression of how a society wants an individual remembered, and shapes each member's ideas of how he or she will be remembered. Failure to perform such rituals threatens both the memories of the individual and the identities of survivors.

Ritualization of death provides a context for the reconstruction and maintenance of a final identity to which the deceased can no longer make a direct contribution. Before concluding our discussion of identity after death (PMI), let us examine how identity *in* death becomes the final touch on the portrait of the self.

2. Death identity: The final touch: When a human organism dies, a new and distinctive identity is added to the deceased's identity repertoire. It is the death identity, or the self as situated in a physically dead and still present body. Identity is a structural concept to the extent that it refers to our location in a social world, and a processual concept since that location is typically defined in terms of ongoing interactional processes of identification (Strauss 1959; Stone 1962). When a person dies, she or he takes on a death identity as others place the person into that social category by enacting his or her final bodily identity. Structurally, we are identified as dead because we no longer hold a place as a psychological social agent among the living. Processually, the death identity is conferred upon us because we can no longer participate in any interactional situation requiring a living response. It would appear that taking on a death identity represents a paradox: Placement is contingent upon what we no longer are or can no longer do; we are merely present bodily, though dead.

Death identity represents more than just a final categorization, however; at least two other functions are served by the conferring of such an identity. First, one's death identity becomes the final touch on the individual's physical appearance. The literature on death and dying in American culture emphasizes the techniques employed to mask death and mirror an image of the self in life (Mitford 1963). Much of the funeral work surrounding the ritualization of death is oriented toward the successful restoration of the body so that the self in death resembles the self in life as closely as possible.

American culture is characterized by heroic attempts to remove the shroud of death from the physical appearance of the decaying organism. The increased number of funeral directors and the perfection of embalming techniques point to the shift from mere preservation of bodily remains to new strategies for restoration and cosmetic re-creation (Habenstein and Lamers 1960; Gorer 1965). When restoration of the physical appearance is not practical or possible, public viewing and open casket visitation are typically replaced by closed casket visitations and/or memorial services in the absence of the body.

In other cultures, there may be little if any attempt to create an appearance of life in the dead. The Japanese, for example, create a death-identity that is anything but lifelike. The face of the deceased is painted white, the head is shaved, and the body is almost always cremated. Viewing only the face through a small opening in the coffin lid is limited to immediate relatives and closest friends (Habenstein and Lamers 1960).

In Western culture, the death identity is a direct reflection of our efforts to deny death. As Pine (1975:21) explains: "Embalming includes dressing the body and restoring it (applying cosmetics) in an attempt to render the deceased lifelike and socially presentable for a public appearance." Within a dramaturgical framework, death identity becomes a socially constructed character that is a complementary but distinctive aspect of the self situated in a carefully staged and orchestrated final performance, and appearances are centrally important (cf. Goffman 1959; Stone 1962). However, the physical performer has no direct, and only marginally indirect, involvement in the impression of the character on the audience. Thus, for the actor in death, the staging and interaction surrounding the performance become the responsibility of the funeral *directors,* family *consultants,* floral *arrangers,* and viewing *audience* – each a dramaturgical team surrounding an inert, dead performer.

Death identity serves a second function as a final touch on the self. As noted previously, there is a chasm created by death that disrupts the continuity of social life. Although the body ceases to exist as a viable organism, the multiplicity of identities that comprise the self continues to have an effect on the social relationships, interactions, and everyday lives of survivors.

How long it takes to resume the business of everyday life, and how that life changes due to the intervention of death, depends upon the degree to which the death identity leads to closure with the living identities of the deceased. An American cultural theme seems to be that the closer the similarity between appearance in death and appearance in life, the sooner and easier the return to normalcy. Conversely, the more the death identity contradicts the living appearance of the deceased, the longer the interruption of typical interaction patterns. American identity emphasizes youth, life, achievement, and recognition here and now.

We conclude that death identity constitutes a delicate thread that pulls together the social space of relationships between individuals before and after death. It bridges a gap created by physical demise; and while the body is susceptible to deterioration and decay, the self as a social essence continues to influence and shape the interaction of survivors. This continuity of social existence is evidenced by the objectification of the self into a new social essence: postmortem identity.

Postmortem identity as a construct

Simply defined, postmortem identity refers to self's identity after the death and disposal of the body. The concept is absent from sociological psychology as far as we know. It speaks, however, to a fundamental issue confronting researchers dealing with the continuity of social existence. Identities are distinctively human, and they affect social relationships regardless of physical presence at, or conscious involvement in, interaction.

We know of no more appropriate example of the transcendent nature of identities in everyday life than the existence and influence of identities beyond death. *Postmortem identity* is used as a technical term for describing the social essence of the self after death. The following sections present a preliminary model of PMI and discuss its genesis as a reconstruction project for identity maintenance by survivors.

1. The conceptual model: The notion of a postmortem identity is fruitfully addressed by Maines (1978) in his discussion of identities without bodies. For example, he states that when a person dies:

The demographer will subtract one person from the population; but, again, because of the failure to see people as social objects, he will overlook the fact that *the deceased person's identity remains in the population.* Friends and relatives remember the person, take him into account, talk about him, mourn him, and sometimes even celebrate his birthday. In this sense, it is clear that such identities continue to have an impact upon social relationships involving the living. (1978: 243, italics his)

The dialectic of bodies and identities, or physical and social dimensions of existence, exemplifies the transcendent nature of self and our efforts to identify individuals. As Maines contends, it is possible to have identities without bodies, just as it is plausible to have bodies without identities. The latter, bodies without identities, indicates major breakdowns in the identity process that typically grounds identities in names. As a result, few bodies exist without a defined or meaningful relationship to the larger social order (Foote 1951). The key is found in the word "meaningful." Although victims of natural disasters, torture beyond recognition, political kidnappings, and war have been categorized as "unidentified persons," flood victims, *desaparecidos* or "disappeareds," or "unknown soldiers," those bodies would not be meaningful for social interaction among those who knew the unidentified individual if there were no PMI. Although these persons were part of the social order when alive, we are now unable to activate the normal interactional involvement that typically gives biographical meaning to their lives. These instances underscore the normal social preoccupation with finding a social niche for the body through naming. Part of the pain for survivors of a person "missing in action" or "disappeared" is that they do not know which identity to bestow on the absent self. The memories of those who disappear may continue to motivate intimates and associates, but the unidentified bodies must be transformed into photos, songs, relics, or other symbols if they are to remain socially real for extended periods of time.

The existence of identities without bodies is a more normal part of society. It can be argued that such identities at some time had to be oriented toward actual or anticipated bodies. But our emphasis is on the fact that these identities are socially real without embodiment. We can act toward them as meaningfully and as frequently as we do other identities that are embodied, just as pious Christians of the twenty-first century may respond to the image of Jesus on a cross. Researchers have documented situations where identities without bodies, or postmortem identities, have influenced individuals and institutions, organized collectivities, attained sainthood, and symbolized social movements (George and George 1955; Hoebel and Jennings 1966; Weinstein and Bell 1982). The general notion of PMI is not new, although its conceptual development has been overlooked by students of sociological psychology. Classical symbolic interactionists view human beings as social objects, and society as the organization of identities (see Znaniecki 1965). As Simmel observed (1950: 410): "Man does not end with the limits of his body or the area comprising his immediate activity."

2. PMI as a reconstruction project: Many examples illustrate postmortem identity as a reconstruction project. Amost two hundred years after his death, George

Washington was promoted to the rank of five-star general (General of the Army). Over one hundred years after the end of the Civil War, Robert E. Lee was pardoned for his activities in the secession of the Confederate states. The Catholic Church lifted its excommunication of Martin Luther and confers sainthood on persons long after death. Deceased persons have had their citizenship stripped from them or citizen status conferred posthumously; court convictions have been overturned or pardons granted after the prisoners have died; and recently the court martial of Private Eddie Slovak, the only soldier to be executed for desertion in World War II, came under judicial review. Despite the absence of a body, identities such as these are reshaped by contemporary society. We define the process of reshaping and reorienting identity after death as *reconstruction*. This is consistent with a social constructionist view, in that beyond death individuals can no longer directly determine their identities, although their identities continue to be determined by others, or forgotten completely – the ultimate social death. Consequently, reconstruction becomes imperative at the point of death in order to maintain the identities of the deceased survivors at least through the transition period.

The PMI reconstruction project begins at the point of physical death (D. Teitge 1981), when survivors begin to resurrect his or her social character and piece together a composite self through reminiscence and the exchange of information. The product of that effort becomes representative of the objectified self in death that survivors remember, talk about, mourn the loss of, and otherwise include in their social interactions.

Over time, two phenomena concerning PMI can be observed. First, the composite identity of the deceased is subject to modification and revision. Changes in the PMI usually result from:

1. New information about the character of the deceased based on his or her decisions prearranged but not known or carried out until after death, such as dispositions of property designated in a will or provision of a trust fund for future heirs
2. New information about the deceased obtained from others acquainted with his or her life identities, such as that provided by co-workers, childhood friends, or old relatives
3. Changes in social institutions or organizational structures that directly or indirectly affect the PMI, such as the modified identity of Captain Bligh based on new evidence by revisionist historians (Maines, 1978)
4. A person's reinterpretation of the deceased's role in his or her life – for example, the life review of elderly persons may significantly reinterpret a long-dead parent's or child's role

A second phenomenon is a gradual decline in the prominence the deceased's PMI may have in the everyday activities of survivors. In other words, with the passage of time there is a tendency for the PMI of the deceased to become less important than other everyday experiences or acquaintances. In some cases, survivors attempt to ignore the PMI of the individual who has died, only to have it reemerge as a result of some special occasion, significant event, or important date. The PMI never disappears until all records or artifacts of the "existence" of the individual disappear, including vestigia or footprints that may be millions of years old, although PMI may be reduced to no more than a historical artifact located in archival data; for example, the archival function of the family for identities during life can be extended to postlife, such as ancestor worship (cf. Weigert and Hastings 1977).

Efforts toward reconstruction of PMI are facilitated by the ritualization of death. Funerals serve as the event for the final appearance of the physical self; and that appearance contributes to the intensity and direction that reconstruction of the deceased's PMI will take. At the same time, the death ritual provides the opportunity for survivors to congregate and participate in the reconstruction project. It is typically at the funeral home, church, public visitations, memorial service, or wake that information about the type and nature of relationships with the deceased is exchanged. The information communicated becomes data, interpreted by survivors and integrated with previous personal knowledge. The product of the synthesis becomes the substance of the PMI that is maintained and transmitted in the future. As new information becomes available, or old data are reevaluated, the PMI is modified. Also, as we noted, the specificity of the identity and the intensity with which it is described tend to become muted with the passage of time.

Summary

This chapter focused on the development of a theoretical framework for conceptualizing identities that exist outside the traditional embodied lifecourse of individuals. We introduce the notions of prenatal identity (PNI) and postmortem identity (PMI) as suggestive constructs in search of further empirical validation as social constructions of an individual's meaning. Although our initial discussion merely begins to codify phenomena already under investigation, we hope that future research will include PNI and PMI as technical terms and sociological psychological variables in deeper interpretations of the perennial issue of human identity, its construction and maintenance.

The discussion of prenatal and postmortem identity illustrates our theoretical orientation to identity as a social construction. The reality of pregnancy identities, identity-bestowing medical technology, and perinatal mourning add flesh and bone, as it were, to the construct of PNI. On the other hand, denial was described as the typical American stance toward death, and the advent of cryonics was cited as evidence of denial efforts. However, the fact remains that, for the time being, death *is* the destiny of each man and woman. Given the inevitability of physical death, and the transcendent nature of social existence, we can reflect on the idea of postmortem identity as the objectification of self victorious, for the moment at least, over death.

5. Identity in a pluralistic society: some parting words

This chapter brings to an end our beginning treatment of identity. An ending is not closure; indeed, an ending may be more of a beginning, and that is the spirit we hope to communicate here. If we are anywhere close to the mark in insisting that identity is a central and characteristic issue in contemporary pluralistic societies, then even our halting, but we think suggestive, development is not only worthwhile, but also an endorsement to thinkers and researchers concerned with identity now and in the future. The best we could hope for our own efforts is that they quickly be superseded by the work of others.

It is in the spirit of making it easier to go beyond our work that we present the three parts of this final chapter. First, we briefly recapitulate the main theoretical and empirical themes. These themes are spun out of the guiding thesis that identity is a socially constructed reality and out of what we see as the underlying paradigm of all sociological psychologists who study identity – namely, social organization structures identity organization. Secondly, assuming the validity of the main arguments, what generic responses are available to individuals and groups in pluralistic societies in which identity issues are characteristic, problematic, and painful? What partial and tantalizing light does a sociological psychological approach to identity throw on the perennial question of authentic human existence and the "true" self? These are the kinds of boundary questions a sociological psychology of identity raises in a compelling and, we think, particularly contemporary cast. Finally, we end the chapter by pointing out further theoretical and empirical directions that seem especially fruitful.

Recapitulation

We began our discussion of the concept of identity by tracing its emergence over a forty-year period. From its initial formulation in the writings of Erik Erikson in the mid 1940s, identity was quickly adopted by psychoanalysts, social psychologists, and sociologists; by both critics and defenders of contemporary American society, though it developed mainly in the hands of critics; and eventually by the general American public. By the end of the 1970s, "identity" was

115

a cultural buzzword often coupled with "crisis," as well as a technical term in social psychology. We know of no other concept that emerged so rapidly and visibly both as a technical term and stock cultural coin.

In Chapter 2, we took the next step toward applicable sociological theory by locating the concept of identity as central to a sociological psychology. This step elaborated upon the pragmatic social constructionist paradigm for developing a theory of identity. The elaboration followed mainly from the theoretical work of symbolic interactionists and social phenomenologists who continue to address the age-old seminal question, Who am I? We started by unpacking variants of the seminal question to sensitize us to the complexity of identity issues often masked by language. A series of propositions then moved from statements about meaning and self as emergent in interaction to a definition of identity as meaningful structures of self. Issues such as multiple identities, identity salience, and emotions were briefly addressed from the growing literature available within sociological psychology.

The propositional discussion helps to codify material about identity as a socially constructed reality and brings us closer to the point of formulating testable models and hypotheses. The broad inclusiveness and elusive definition and operationalization of identity are unavoidable features of a general and effective definition of self. Nevertheless, we see some crucial issues concerning identity that deserve further attention from scholars:

1.   The dialectic of subjective and objective identities as a matrix of existential meaning and the problematic of human alienation
2.   The content of sociohistorically available identities as a link between sociological psychology and the larger sweep of historical interpretation
3.   The organization of multiple identities as a defining characteristic of the psychology of contemporary pluralistic societies
4.   The spatiotemporal continuity of identity as a definitive problem in contemporary societies
5.   The relationship between identity and emotions as a telling interpretive key for making sense out of the sensibilities of our age

The propositional outline and suggested thematic concerns of a theory of identity set the stage for application to substantive areas of research. Empirical applications allow us to gauge the initial fruitfulness of a pragmatic social constructionist paradigm both in deepening our understanding and in testing particular formulations.

The second step from theoretical foundations toward the interpretation of empirical issues requires the formulation of middle-range theories and testable models or hypotheses. Chapter 3 selectively applied identity theory to bodies available for interpretation. A primary and fateful interpretation of bodies imposes gender as a socially constructed reality. The first part of the discussion emphasized the definition of humans as biologically or socially different; that is, the distinction between sex as a biological referent and gender as a social referent. The interpretive power of identity theory was exemplified through the analysis it makes possible of transsexualism and homosexuality as particularly instructive variations in gender identity. The project was taken another step with the construction of a modest middle-range theory aimed at the formulation of testable hypotheses concerning selected links between homosexual identity and occupations. The formulations center around the perennial issue of human realization or estrangement at both the subjective and societal levels of identity integration. In this way, the general issue of multiple identities was investigated in the relationships among sexual identity, occupational location, and identity integration. The effort to formulate a middle-range set of propositions illustrates that there is no a priori contradiction between a pragmatic social constructionist paradigm and axiomatic or theory-building tactics for further articulating the theory and moving toward empirical applications, as long as researchers are sensitive to the difference between explanation and understanding.

After the rather standard effort of Chapter 3, the next chapter moved into the speculative but, we feel, exciting direction of types of identities without bodies. Chapter 4 is our favorite chapter, and we hope a stimulating one. The social constructionist paradigm is conclusively if only partly (as is always the case), validated by the existence and definition of identities in the absence of bodies or of independently functioning bodies.

Working from the distinction between bodies and identities, we summarized some of the writings on identities bestowed before birth, or prenatal identities (PNI). PNI is an identity construction project in which a fetal organism is given meaning and an imputed identity that functions to organize the responses of others even before that organism is outside the mother's body or test tube. The PNI is replaced by a postpartum or neonate identity at the event of birth. At birth, PNI is modified as the socially unembodied self becomes a sociohistorically available and interactionally validated actor who is now bodily situated in contexts of public social structure and interactional encounters. The meaning of PNI, such as a desired or undesired pregnancy, affects the initial identities bestowed on the neonate. Thus, PNI marks the beginning of lifelong identity construction projects.

At the polar extreme from PNI is postmortem identity (PMI). PMI is the identity or series of identities reconstructed after the biological death of the organism. Working from a historical perspective, we see denial as a typical response to death, particularly in contemporary America. Denial of death appears to be a typical attitude of individuals, as well as a core value institutionalized in the funerary industry. To grasp this aspect of human life, we formulated PMI as the product of strategies by which the individual, survivors, or institutions work to bestow a form of life after death on the individual. PMI was interpreted as a reconstruction project by which a new and meaningful identity is attached to the memory of an individual who is no longer active in the identity-construction processes.

One of the more illustrative and contemporary PMI tactics available to individuals and survivors is made possible by the application of enabling technology such as cryonics. Belief in the life-sustaining capacities of frozen bodies enables dying individuals, survivors, and a new line of business to traffic in reconstructed PMIs. More traditional means such as funerary cosmetics were also discussed as a part of the production of PMI that can be handed down as archival data sustaining identities after death, both of the deceased and of survivors.

The discussion of prenatal and postmortem identities attempts to codify phenomena already investigated by others, and to extend the application of identity as a social construction beyond the physical life of the individual. The viability and usefulness of PNI and PMI as interpretive concepts serve as exemplars for the validity of the social constructionist paradigm. We would hope that PNI and PMI may serve well in future studies as both interpretive concepts and empirical variables.

Generic responses to the identity issue

If we grant even partial validity to the social construction of identity theme, the question naturally arises of individual and group responses to the forces shaping identity in today's world. Leaving aside such large-scale events as thermonuclear disaster, revolutions, and overt ethnic conflict, we would like to sketch selected generic responses to the centrality of identity dynamics in postmodern societies. Within modern America, for example, we can point to empirical patterns reflecting the complex foundations of identity. The social structural imperatives of associational, cognitive, and actional pluralism generate a complex set of identities. Furthermore, the underlying normative substructure of perennial and deeply encoded cultural imperatives concerning identity appear to be changing rapidly enough to affect individuals in a historically new way during the course of one lifetime. Examples of traditionally bedrock identities now open to change during a person's lifetime are gender, age, and national, political, ethnic, and religious categories.

The increase in rates of change in technological and social factors translates into an increased tempo of identity construction and negotiation. How may contemporaries respond to the sociocultural pluralism so that they continue to sustain a sufficiently integrated and continuous sense of identity for organizing and motivating their lives? We would like to touch on a variety of generic responses. First, contemporaries can seek meaning in impulse or personal fulfillment and abandon institutions to mere rote enactment or more or less coercive patterns of behavior (Turner 1976). They would be the confident self-seekers who can make it on their own. Second, contemporaries can acquire multiple identities and a mutable sense of self that easily migrates from one kind of identity to another as circumstances suggest (Zurcher 1977). There is no transsituational commitment to conventional identities or traditional values. These motile solutions are not likely to supply the stability that comes from plausibility structures that last throughout the life course; nor do they offer strong networks of commitment that come from external structures and cultural traditions.

A third response would be to adhere to traditional values and the historical institutions transmitting these values through the teaching of clear and simple behavioral and motivational norms, such as institutional religions (see Kilpatrick 1975). Such motivation partly explains the strength of evangelical Christianity and fundamentalist politics in the postmodern mentality of contemporary America. A fourth possibility offers strong structure and encompassing commitment for those willing to encyst themselves within ideological enclaves of sectarian religious, political, countercultural, or paramilitaristic groups that "greedily" demand total commitment and extensive temporal involvement (Coser 1974).

This encysting solution reintroduces "naturalness" to the experience of personal identity with greater intensity than naturally occurs in mundane society. Such encysted naturalness faces special problems of social and cognitive engineering, since the encysted person may always remember when his or her massively natural current identity was not yet, and there are always witnesses of earlier days who can attest to such preexistent identities. Examples of relevant cases abound, from the case of a kidnapped celebrity to young people attracted to cults or sects, only to be kidnapped by parents and "deprogrammed."

A fifth possible response is more likely a question and perhaps an idea. Can it be that a historically new dynamic is emerging within consciousness that demands a new mode and source of identity as well? Is it possible for humans to accept and sustain an identity taken as typical and natural, while at the same time have that identity grounded in a dialectical and reflexive consciousness that indeed the identity is socially constructed? Can a religious devotee, for example, remain faithful and yet recognize the contingent social and psychological origins, functions, and content of his or her religious identity? Can continuous reflexivity and self-criticism be institutionalized in society and internalized in experience, and yet provide an encoded rule for contemporary identity (see Zaner 1974)? To paraphrase the title of an article addressed to this general issue, "Can continual reflexivity be institutionalized?'' (see Berger 1967:191). And if some members of society attain critical and reflexive identities, could all or even typical members of society acquire them? Finally, can such a continually reflexive identity fulfill the functions of identity as a natural meaning – namely, to anchor a sense of selfhood, authenticity, stability, and lifelong continuity without empty narcissism or fatuous self-searching (cf. Lasch 1979)? This is a central question and one that a sociological psychology raises with full force.

As we finish this brief listing of generic responses to contemporary identity issues, we would like to mention an emerging concept that we think helps us understand contemporary identity. That concept is *sociological ambivalence*. From the early work of Robert Merton to more recent applications to the identity and motivation of groups ranging from scientists to orthodox Jews, ambivalence seems particularly powerful for analyzing identity in a pluralistic and changing society (see Goffman 1963; Mitroff 1974; Merton 1976; Heilman 1977). Identity ambivalence is a corollary of multiple identities in the context of social change. Sociological ambivalence is well able to address one of the defining characteristics of contemporary identity and offers promise of important theoretical and empirical development. This brings us to our final word.

Past and future directions

Identity is the topic of this book. We did not intend a complete discussion of its emergence, foundations, articulation, and empirical possibilities. Nor did we develop a cultural interpretation of the meaning of identity in contemporary America. Rather, we hoped to touch on these projects and sketch beginnings in each of them. The vast expanse of scholarly and popular writings on identity cannot be handled adequately in a single volume. We chose to start with a brief historical tracing of the emergence of identity as a technical term, and then we shifted to a selective codification of theoretical terms and propositions of the mainlines of identity scholarship within traditions forming the recently self-conscious discipline of sociological psychology. We like to think that these beginning efforts are as much a part of the development of sociological psychology as a contribution to identity studies. We are not fooled, however, into believing that the widespread use of identity implies agreement on its meaning or even a clear understanding of its various meanings (see the variation of meanings in Mackenzie 1978; Tajfel 1982; Breakwell 1983).

Throughout most of the theoretical developments and empirical, applications, we took the stance of interpreting and explaining identity. Identity is the effect, the dependent variable, the concept to be unpacked. It goes without saying that an adequate identity theory must also investigate identity as cause, independent variable, interpretive concept. Identity channels behavior, and multiple identities may generate a sense of well-being (see Stryker and Serpe 1982; Thoits 1983).

Only a full dialectical model or set of propositions that explains identity as well as using it to explain other phenomena would constitute an identity theory worthy of the name. For example, we need to study how identities, once formed, provide motivational schema and felt values that direct the way in which individuals live, decide, suffer, and dream. Upwardly mobile individuals working out their lives as successful, wealthy, and powerful persons are striving in the service of a typical American identity. Unfortunately, self-conscious individuals trapped by inadequate diet, lack of education, and poverty are also all too typically American. Others seek to fulfill identities as revolutionaries, ascetics, communards, heros, aesthetes, or athletes; and they may shape the most counterconventional life-styles in pursuit of their identity projects.

Identities, like all socially constructed realities, are structured with internal logics of action, thought, and feeling that direct behavior, interpret experience, and provide the only materials individuals have for making sense out of their lives. Identity theory may be fruitfully applied to such phenomena as charismatic leaders and exceptional actors in the dramas of history. The plausibility of psychohistory would be strengthened by the application of sociological psychological categories. The effect of heroic identities shaping the course of events is a necessary part of an adequate understanding of history, as is the functioning of plebeian identities in the stuff of history.

A continuing program to develop identity theory would have to include at least four levels of investigation. First, there is the biographical level of identity formation, change, transition, and reconstruction throughout the life course. Quite likely, this is the point of origin for the rapid emergence of identity from the work of psychoanalysts on the issue of infant identification with parents. Second, identities may be studied as they are enacted and as they function at the situational level. Situational analysis is the explicit focus of much social psychological work, and it is perhaps the most technically sophisticated and amenable to quantitative transformation of data as well as observational methods.

Third, there is the group and institutional level at which identities are formed and enacted in terms of more or less formally defined positions. It is here that the rather recently codified work of sociological psychologists can make a significant contribution. The negotiations and links between dominant institutional forms and identity are fraught with important lessons. Consider such forms as bureaucracy, education, ethnicity, automation, nuclear militarism, democracy, or computer technology, and pair them with types of identity. The issues of identity formation and maintenance are shared by totalitarian regimes and democratic societies, although the empirical patterns and structures are different. Indeed, the very survival of each type of system demands adequate identity formation and control, and one of the dilemmas of democracy is how to achieve these necessary identities while safeguarding the appropriately named antinomian principle of individual freedom and self-determination. The application of identity theory to contemporary democracy promises to deepen our understanding of both.

The fourth level concerns historical and cultural identity codes and contents. To our way of thinking, this is both the most difficult to investigate and also the final assessment of the epistemological validity of identity theory: It must make human history more transparent to ourselves. Finally, out of the illumination gained from understanding identity at these four levels, we hope that identity theory would make a contribution to perennial queries about authentic and genuine knowledge of self, about the difference between the surface and deeper meanings of life, and about the very possibility of understanding the human condition. Erikson himself states that "existential identity has to emerge from the psychological identity" (1983: 27). At this point in our reflection, existential inquiry merges with regnant dicta of Western civilization – namely, that humans are images of God, and the human task is to know thyself.

The longer hope of this book is that its tentative formulations will further the interdisciplinary impetus that attended the scholarly birth of the concept of identity in the first place. The theoretical framework provides a turf on which humanists, clinicians, and social and behavioral scientists can meet within a relevant universe of discourse. In the even longer run, such dialogue would inform the very encoding of our culture itself, thus raising the level of self-awareness historically available to those who come after us. Of course, it remains to be seen how far the crucial issue of self-understanding will be illuminated for, and put to the service of, human life by the development of identity theory. We believe the effort is a defining feature of our times.

Bibliography

Aldous, Joan, 1978. *Family Careers.* New York: Wiley.

Alexander, C. N., Jr., and M. G. Wiley, 1981. "Situated activity and identity formation." In Morris Rosenberg and Ralph H. Turner (eds.), *Social Psychology.* New York: Basic Books, pp. 269–89.

Antonio, R. J., 1972. "The processual dimension of degradation ceremonies: the Chicago conspiracy trial: success or failure?" *British Journal of Sociology* 23 (September): 287–97.

Aries, Phillipe, 1974. *Western Attitudes Toward Death: From the Middle Ages to the Present.* Baltimore: Johns Hopkins University Press.

Barber, Bernard, 1983. *The Logic and Limits of Trust.* New Brunswick, NJ: Rutgers University Press.

Becker, Ernest, 1975. *The Denial of Death.* New York: Free Press.

Becker, Howard S., 1960. "Notes on the concept of commitment." *American Journal of Sociology* 66: 32–40.

Becker, Howard S., Blanche Geer, Everett C. Hughes, and Anselm L. Strauss, 1961. *Boys in White.* Chicago: University of Chicago Press.

Bell, Alan P., and Martin S. Weinberg, 1978. *Homosexualities: A Study of Diversity Among Men and Women.* New York: Simon and Schuster.

Bellah, Robert N., 1968. "Identity." *International Encyclopedia of the Social Sciences.* New York: Macmillan.

———, 1970. *Beyond Belief.* New York: Harper and Row.

———, 1978. *The Broken Covenant.* New York: Seabury.

Bensman, Joseph, and Robert Lilienfeld, 1979. *Between Public and Private.* New York: Free Press.

Berger, Peter L., 1963. *Invitation to Sociology.* New York: Anchor.

———, 1966. "Identity as a problem in the sociology of knowledge." *European Journal of Sociology* 7: 105–15.

———, 1967. *The Sacred Canopy.* Garden City, NY: Doubleday.

———, 1981. Personal correspondence.

Berger, P. L., and H. Kellner, 1964. "Marriage and the construction of reality." *Diogenes* 46: 1–25.

Berger, Peter L., and Thomas Luckmann, 1966. *The Social Construction of Reality.* Garden City, NY: Doubleday.

Berger, Peter L., Brigitte Berger, and Hansfried Kellner, 1973. *The Homeless Mind.* New York: Random House.

Bettelheim, Bruno, 1967. *The Empty Fortress.* New York: Free Press.

Biddle, Bruce J., 1979. *Role Theory: Expectations, Identities, and Behaviors.* New York: Academic Press.

Blau, Peter, and Otis Dudley Duncan, 1967. *The American Occupational Structure.* New York: Wiley.

Blauner, Robert, 1966. "Death and the social structure." *Psychiatry* 29: 378–394.

Blumer, Herbert, 1969. *Symbolic Interactionism: Perspective and Method.* Englewood Cliffs, NJ: Prentice-Hall.

Blumstein, P. W., 1973. "Audience, Machiavellianism, and tactics of identity bargaining." *Sociometry* 36: 346–65.

Bowman, LeRoy, 1959. *The American Funeral*. Washington, DC: Public Affairs Press.

Breakwell, Glynis M. (ed.), 1983. *Threatened Identities*. New York: Wiley.

Brim, Orville G. (ed.), 1970. *The Dying Patient*. New York: Russell Sage.

Burke, Kenneth, 1965. *Permanence and Change*. Indianapolis: Bobbs-Merrill.

Burke, Peter J., 1980. "The self: Measurement requirements from an interactionist perspective." *Social Psychology Quarterly* 43: 18–29.

Cassel, Eric J., 1974. "Dying in a technological society." In Peter Steinfels and Robert Veatch (eds.), *Death Inside Out*. New York: Harper and Row.

Chafetz, Janet Saltzman, 1978. *Masculine/Feminine or Human?* (2nd ed.). Itasca, IL: Peacock.

Charmaz, Kathy, 1980. *The Social Reality of Death*. Reading, MA: Addison-Wesley.

Chickering, Arthur W., 1969. *Education and Identity*. San Francisco: Jossey-Bass.

Coan, Richard W., 1977. *Hero, Artist, Sage, or Saint?* New York: Columbia University Press.

Cohen, Stanley, and Laurie Taylor, 1978. *Escape Attempts*. New York: Penguin.

Coser, Lewis A., 1974. *Greedy Institutions*. New York: Free Press.

Cottrell, Leonard S., 1969. "Interpersonal interaction and the development of the self." In David Goslin (ed.), *Handbook of Socialization Theory and Research*. Chicago: University of Chicago Press.

Dailey, Charles A., 1971. *Assessment of Lives: Personality Evaluation in a Bureaucratic Society*. San Francisco: Jossey-Bass.

Dashefsky, Arnold (ed.), 1976. *Ethnic Identity in American Society*. Chicago: Rand McNally.

Davidson, Laurie, and Laura K. Gordon, 1979. *The Sociology of Gender*. Chicago: Rand McNally.

Davis, Fred, 1979. *Yearning for Yesterday*. New York: Free Press.

De Levita, David J., 1965. *The Concept of Identity*. New York: Basic Books.

Dempsey, David, 1975. *The Way We Die: An Investigation of Death and Dying in America Today*. New York: McGraw-Hill.

Devins, Gerald M., and Robert T. Diamond, 1977. "The determination of death." *Omega* 7: 277–96.

Douglas, Jack D., F. Adler, P. Adler, A. Fontana, C. Freeman, and J. Kotarba, 1980. *Introduction to the Sociologies of Everyday Life*. Boston: Allyn and Bacon.

Dumont, Richard G., and Dennis O. Foss, 1973. *The American View of Death: Acceptance or Denial?* Cambridge, MA: Schenkman.

Duncan, James S. (ed.), 1982. *Housing and Identity*. New York: Holmes and Meier.

du Preez, Peter, 1980. *The Politics of Identity*. New York: St. Martin's Press.

Erikson, Erik, 1946. "Ego development and historical change." *Psychoanalytic Study of the Child* 2: 359–96.

———, 1950. *Childhood and Society*. New York: Norton.

———, 1956. "The problem of ego identity." *Journal of the American Psychoanalytic Association* 4: 56–121.

———, 1958. *Young Man Luther*. New York: Norton.

———, 1959. *Identity and the Life Cycle: Selected Papers by Erik H. Erikson. Psychological Issues*. Vol. 1. New York: International Universities Press.

———, 1968. *Identity: Youth and Crisis*. New York: Norton.

———, 1968a. "Identity, Psychosocial." *International Encyclopedia of the Social Sciences*. New York: Macmillan.

———, 1974. *Dimensions of a New Identity*. New York: Norton.

———, 1978. *Adulthood*. New York: Norton. (edited)

———, 1981. Personal correspondence.

———, 1983. "A conversation with Erik Erikson." *Psychology Today* 17: 22–30.

Ettinger, Richard C. W., 1964. *The Prospect of Immortality*. Garden City, NY: Doubleday.

Farberow, Norman L., 1966. *Taboo Topics*. New York: Atherton.

Faunce, W. A., and Robert L. Fulton, 1958. "The sociology of death: A neglected area of research." *Social Forces* 36: 205–9.

Feifel, Herman (ed.), 1959. *The Meaning of Death*. New York: McGraw-Hill.

———, 1977. *New Meanings of Death*. New York: McGraw-Hill.

Feinbloom, D., 1976. *Transvestites and Transsexuals: Mixed Views*. New York: Delacorte.

Feldman, S. D., 1979. "Nested identities." In Norman K. Denzin (ed.), *Studies in Symbolic Interaction*, Vol. II. Greenwich, CT: JAI Press, pp. 399–418.

Finkelstein, J., 1980. "Considerations for a sociology of the emotions." In Norman K. Denzin (ed.), *Studies in Symbolic Interaction*, Vol. III. Greenwich, CT: JAI Press, pp. 111–21.

Foote, Nelson N., 1951. "Identification as the basis for a theory of motivation." *American Sociological Review* 16: 14–21.

———, 1981. Personal correspondence.

Foote, Nelson N., and Leonard S. Cottrell, Jr., 1955. *Identity and Interpersonal Competence*. Chicago: University of Chicago Press.

Fox, Renee C., 1959. *Experiment Perilous*. Glencoe, IL: Free Press.

Fromm, Erich, 1941. *Escape from Freedom*. New York: Rinehart.

Fulton, Robert, 1961. "Discussion of a symposium on attitudes toward death in older persons." *Journal of Gerontology* 16: 44–66.

——— (ed.), 1965. *Death and Identity*. New York: Wiley.

———, 1967. "The denying of death." In Earl Grollman (ed.), *Explaining Death to Children*. Boston: Beacon Press.

Fulton, Robert, and Julie Fulton, 1971. "A psychosocial aspect of terminal care: Anticipatory grief." *Omega* 2: 91–100.

Gagnon, John H., and William Simon, 1973. *Sexual Conduct*. Chicago: Aldine.

Garfinkel, Harold, 1956. "Conditions of successful degradation ceremonies." *American Journal of Sociology* 61: 420–24.

———, 1967. *Studies in Ethnomethodology*. Englewood Cliffs, NJ: Prentice-Hall.

Gecas, V., 1982. "The self concept." *Annual Review of Sociology* 8: 1–33.

Gecas, V., D. L. Thomas, and A. J. Weigert, 1973. "Social identities in Anglo and Latin adolescents." *Social Forces* 51: 477–84.

George, K., and C. H. George, 1955. "Roman Catholic sainthood and social status: A statistical and analytic study." *Journal of Religion* 35: 85–98.

Gerth, Hans, and C. Wright Mills, 1964. *Character and Social Structure*. New York: Harcourt, Brace and World. Originally published in 1953.

Glaser, Barney G., and Anselm L. Strauss, 1964. "Awareness contexts and social interaction." *American Sociological Review* 19: 669–79.

Glassner, William, 1972. *The Identity Society*. New York: Harper and Row.

Glazer, Nathan, and Daniel P. Moynihan (eds.), 1975. *Ethnicity: Theory and Experience*. Cambridge, MA: Harvard University Press.

Gleason, Phillip, 1983. "Identifying identity: A semantic history." *Journal of American History* 69: 910–31.

Goffman, Erving, 1959. *The Presentation of Self in Everyday Life*. Garden City, NY: Anchor Books.

———, 1961. *Asylums*. Garden City, NY: Doubleday Anchor.

———, 1961a. *Encounters*. Indianapolis: Bobbs-Merrill.

———, 1963. *Stigma: Notes on the Management of Spoiled Identity*. Englewood Cliffs, NJ: Prentice-Hall.

———, 1967. *Interaction Ritual*. Garden City, NY: Anchor Books.

———, 1974. *Frame Analysis*. New York: Harper and Row.

Gordon, Chad, 1968. "Self-conceptions: Configurations of content." In Chad Gordon and Kenneth J. Gergen (eds.), *The Self in Social Interaction*. New York: Wiley, pp. 115–36.

———, 1976. "Development of evaluated role identities." In Alex Inkeles (ed.), *Annual Review of Sociology,* Vol. 2, Palo Alto: Annual Reviews, Inc., pp. 405–33.

Gordon, Steven L., 1981. "The sociology of sentiments and emotions." In Morris Rosenberg and Ralph H. Turner (eds.), *Social Psychology*. New York: Basic Books, pp. 562–92.

Gorer, Geoffrey, 1965. *Death, Grief, and Mourning*. Garden City, NY: Doubleday.

Gould, R. L., 1972. "The phases of adult life: A study in developmental psychology." *American Journal of Psychiatry* 129: 33–43.

Grollman, Earl A., 1974. *Concerning Death*. Boston: Beacon Press.

Gross, E., and G. Stone, 1964. "Embarrassment and the analysis of role requirements." *American Journal of Sociology* 70: 1–15.

Gubrium, Jaber F., and David R. Buckholdt, 1977. *Toward Maturity*. San Francisco: Jossey-Bass.

Guiot, J. M., 1977. "Attribution and identity construction: Some comments." *American Sociological Review* 42: 692–704.

Gumperz, John T. (ed.), 1982. *Language & Social Identity*. New York: Cambridge University Press.

Habenstein, Robert W., and William M. Lamers, 1960. *Funeral Customs the World Over*. Milwaukee: Bul. Fin. Printers.

Habermas, Jurgen, 1974. "On social identity." *Telos* 19 (Spring): 91–103.

———, 1979. *Communication and the Evolution of Society*. Boston: Beacon Press.

Hadden, S. C., and M. Lester, 1978. "Talking identity: The production of 'self' in interaction." *Human Studies* 1: 331–56.

Harmer, Ruth M., 1963. *The High Cost of Dying*. New York: Collier.

Harré, Rom, 1983. "Identity projects." In G. Breakwell (ed.), *Threatened Identities*. New York: Wiley, pp. 31–51.

Harry, Joseph, and William B. DeVall, 1978. *The Social Organization of Gay Males*. New York: Praeger.

Heilman, S. C., 1977. "Inner and outer identities: Sociological ambivalence among orthodox Jews." *Jewish Social Studies* 39(3): 227–40.

Hepworth, Mike, 1975. *Blackmail*. London: Routledge and Kegan Paul.

Hewitt, John P., 1979. *Self and Society*. Boston: Allyn and Bacon.

Hewitt, J. P., and R. Stokes, 1975. "Disclaimers." *American Sociological Review* 40: 1–11.

Hochschild, Arlie R., 1975. "The sociology of feeling and emotion: Selected possibilities." In Marcia Millman and Rosabeth M. Kanter (eds.), *Another Voice*. Garden City, NY: Anchor.

Hoebel, Edward A., and Jesse D. Jennings (eds.), 1966. *Readings in Anthropology*. New York: McGraw-Hill.

Holland, Ray, 1977. *Self in Social Context*. New York: St. Martin's Press.

Holter, Harriet, 1970. *Sex Roles and Social Structure*. Oslo: Universtitetsforlaget.

Hughes, Everett C., 1971. *The Sociological Eye*. Chicago: Aldine.

Humphreys, Laud, 1971. *Out of the Closets: The Sociology of Homosexual Liberation*. Englewood Cliffs, NJ: Prentice-Hall.

Husserl, Edmund, 1970. *The Crisis of European Sciences and Transcendental Phenomenology: An Introduction to Phenomenological Philosophy*. Evanston, IL: Northwestern.

Ichheiser, Gustav, 1970. *Appearances and Realities: Misunderstanding in Human Relations*. San Francisco: Jossey-Bass.

Institute of Society, Ethics, and the Life Sciences: Task Force on Death and Dying, 1977. "Refinements in the criteria for the determination of death: An appraisal." In Sandra Wilcox and Marilyn Sutton (eds.), *Understanding Death and Dying*. Port Washington, NY: Alfred Publishing.

Jagger, Alison, and Paula R. Struhl, 1977. *Feminist Frameworks*. New York: McGraw-Hill.

Jones, E., A. Kanouse, H. Kelley, R. Nisbett, S. Valins, and B. Weiner, 1971. *Attribution: Perceiving the Causes of Behavior*. Morristown, NJ: General Learning Press.

Kakar, Sudhir (ed.), 1979. *Identity and Adulthood*. New Delhi: Oxford University Press.

Kanter, Rosabeth Moss, 1972. *Commitment and Community*. Cambridge, MA: Harvard University Press.

Kaplan, Alexander G., and Joan P. Bean, 1976. *Beyond Sex-Role Stereotypes*. Boston: Little, Brown.

Kastenbaum, Robert J., 1977. *Death, Society and Human Experience*. St. Louis, MO: Mosby.

Kastenbaum, Robert, and Ruth Aisenberg, 1972. *The Psychology of Death*. New York: Springer.

Katz, J., 1975. "Essences as moral identities." *American Journal of Sociology* 80: 1369–90.

Kavanaugh, Robert E., 1972. *Facing Death*. Baltimore: Penguin.

Kemper, Theodore D., 1978. *A Social Interactional Theory of Emotions*. New York: Wiley.

Kessler, Suzanne J., and Wendy McKenna, 1978. *Gender: An Ethnomethodological Approach*. New York: Wiley.

Kilpatrick, William, 1975. *Identity and Intimacy*. New York: Dell.

Klapp, Orrin E., 1969. *Collective Search for Identity*. New York: Holt, Rinehart and Winston.

Kubler-Ross, Elisabeth, 1975. *Death, The Final Stage of Growth*. Englewood Cliffs, NJ: Prentice-Hall.

Kuhn, M. H., and T. S. McPartland, 1954. "An empirical investigation of self-attitudes." *American Sociological Review* 19: 68–77.

Laing, R. D., 1971. *The Politics of the Family*. New York: Vintage Books.

Lambert, Helen H., 1978. "Biology and equality: A perspective on sex differences." *SIGNS: Journal of Women in Culture and Society* 4(1): 97–117.

Langbaum, Robert, 1977. *The Mysteries of Identity: A Theme in Modern Literature*. New York: Oxford University Press.

Lasch, Christopher, 1979. *The Culture of Narcissism*. New York: Norton.

Levine, Martin P., 1979. *Gay Men: The Sociology of Male Homosexuality*. New York: Harper and Row.

Levinson, Daniel J., 1978. *The Seasons of a Man's Life*. New York: Ballantine Books.

Lewis, J. David, and Richard L. Smith, 1980. *American Sociology and Pragmatism*. Chicago: University of Chicago Press.

Lewis, J. David, and A. J. Weigert, 1985. "Trust as a social reality." *Social Forces* 63: 967–85.

Lichtenstein, Heinz, 1977. *The Dilemma of Human Identity*. New York: Jason Aronson.

Lifton, Robert J., 1976. *The Life of the Self*. New York: Simon and Schuster.

———, 1979. *The Broken Connection*. New York: Simon and Schuster.

Lindesmith, Alfred R., Anselm L. Strauss, and Norman K. Denzin, 1977. *Social Psychology*. New York: Holt, Rinehart and Winston.

Lofland, John, 1969. *Deviance and Identity*. Englewood Cliffs, NJ: Prentice-Hall.

Lofland, Lyn H., 1978. *The Craft of Dying*. Beverly Hills, CA: Sage.

Luckmann, Thomas, 1967. *The Invisible Religion*. New York: Macmillan.

Luckmann, Thomas, and Peter L. Berger, 1964. "Social mobility and personal identity." *European Journal of Sociology* 5: 331–44.

Luhmann, Niklas, 1979. *Trust and Power*. New York: Wiley.

Lynd, Helen M., (1958) 1961. *On Shame and the Search for Identity*. New York: Science Editions.

Mackenzie, W. J., 1978. *Political Identity*. New York: St. Martin's Press.

Maines, D. R. 1978. "Bodies and selves: Notes on a fundamental dilemma in demography." In Norman K. Denzin (ed.), *Studies in Symbolic Interaction*, Vol. I. Greenwich, CT: JAI Press, pp. 241–65.

Malinowski, Bronislaw, 1948. *Magic, Science and Religion*. Boston: Beacon Press.

Mann, Arthur, 1979. *The One and the Many: Reflections on the American Identity.* Chicago: University of Chicago Press.

McCall, George J., and J. L. Simmons, 1966. *Identities and Interactions.* New York: Free Press. Revised edition, 1978.

———, 1982. *Social Psychology: A Sociological Approach.* New York: Free Press.

Mead, George H., 1934. *Mind, Self, and Society.* Chicago: University of Chicago Press.

Meltzer, Bernard N., 1964. "Mead's social psychology." In Jerome Manis and Bernard N. Meltzer (eds.), *Symbolic Interaction: A Reader in Social Psychology.* Boston: Allyn and Bacon.

Meltzer, Bernard N., John W. Petras, and Larry T. Reynolds, 1975. *Symbolic Interactionism: Genesis, Varieties and Criticism.* London: Routledge & Kegan Paul.

Merton, Robert K., 1976. *Sociological Ambivalence.* New York: Free Press.

Messinger, S. D., H. Sampson, and R. D. Towne, 1962. "Life as theater: Some notes on the dramaturgic approach to social reality." *Sociometry* 25: 98–110.

Miller, R. S., 1978. "The social construction and reconstruction of physiological events: Acquiring the pregnancy identity." In Norman K. Denzin (ed.), *Studies in Symbolic Interaction,* Vol. 1. Greenwich, CT: JAI Press, pp. 181–204.

Mills, C. Wright, 1959. *The Sociological Imagination.* New York: Oxford University Press.

Mitford, Jessica, 1963. *The American Way of Death.* NY: Simon and Schuster.

Mitroff, I. I., 1974. "Norms and counternorms in a select group of the Apollo moon scientists: A case study of the ambivalence of scientists." *American Sociological Review* 39: 579–95.

Mol, Hans J., 1976. *Identity and the Sacred.* New York: Free Press.

——— (ed.), 1978. *Identity and Religion: International Cross-Cultural Approaches.* Beverly Hills, CA: Sage.

Money, John, and Anka Ehrhardt, 1972. *Man and Woman, Boy and Girl.* Baltimore: Johns Hopkins University Press.

Morgan, Ernest, 1973. *A Manual of Death Education and Simple Burial.* Burnsville, NC: Celo Press.

Morris, Jan, 1975. *Conundrum.* New York: Signet.

Natanson, Marurice, 1974. *Phenomenology, Role and Reason.* Springfield, IL: Charles C. Thomas.

Oakley, Ann, 1972. *Sex, Gender, and Society.* San Francisco: Harper and Row.

Ortega y Gasset, José, 1961. *The Modern Theme.* New York: Harper Torchbooks.

———, 1963, *Meditations on Quixote.* New York: Norton.

Parkes, Colin, 1972. *Bereavement: Studies of Grief in Adult Life.* New York: International Universities Press.

Parsons, Talcott, 1968. "The position of identity in the general theory of action." In Chad Gordon and Kenneth J. Gergen (eds.), *The Self in Social Interaction.* New York: Wiley, pp. 11–23.

Peppers, Larry G., and Ronald J. Knapp, 1980. *Motherhood and Mourning.* New York: Praeger.

Perry, John (ed.), 1975. *Personal Identity.* Berkeley: University of California Press.

Petras, John W., 1978. *The Social Meaning of Human Sexuality.* Boston: Allyn and Bacon.

Pine, Vanderlyn, 1974. "Dying, death, and social behavior." In Bernard Schoenberg et al. (eds.), *Anticipatory Grief.* New York: Columbia University Press.

———, 1975. *Caretaker of the Dead: The American Funeral Director.* New York: Irvington.

Pine, Vanderlyn, and Derek L. Phillips, 1970. "The cost of dying: A sociological analysis of funeral expenditures." *Social Problems* 17: 405–17.

Ponse, Barbara, 1978. *Identities in the Lesbian World.* Westport, CT: Greenwood Press.

Pye, L., 1960. "Personal identity and political ideology." In Dwaine Marvick (ed.), *Political Decision-Makers.* New York: Free Press, pp. 290–313.

Raether, Howard C., and Robert C. Slater, 1975. *The Funeral Director and His Role as a Counselor.* Milwaukee, WI: National Funeral Directors Association.

Riesman, David, Reuel Denney, and Nathan Glazer, 1950. *The Lonely Crowd.* New Haven, CT: Yale University Press.

Robertson, Roland, and Burkart Holzner (eds.), 1979. *Identity and Authority*. London: Basil-Blackwell.

Rorty, Amelie O. (ed.), 1976. *The Identities of Persons*. Berkley: University of California Press.

Rose, Jerry D., 1980. *Introduction to Sociology*. (4th ed.). Chicago: Rand McNally.

Rosenberg, Morris, and Ralph H. Turner (eds.), 1981. *Social Psychology: Sociological Perspectives*. New York: Basic Books.

Rubin, Lillian B., 1981. *Women of a Certain Age*. New York: Harper Colophon Books.

Ruitenbeek, Hendrik M., 1964. *The Individual and the Crowd: A Study of Identity in America*. New York: Mentor Books.

Sargent, Alice C., 1977. *Beyond Sex Roles*. Boulder, CO: West.

Scheff, T. J., 1970. "On the concepts of identity and social relationship." In Tamotsu Shibutani (ed.), *Human Nature and Collective Behavior*. Englewood Cliffs, NJ: Prentice-Hall, pp. 193–207.

Schein, Edgar H., 1971. *Coercive Persuasion*. New York: Norton.

Schlenker, Barry L., 1980. *Impression Management*. Monterey, CA: Brooks/Cole.

Schmitt, Raymond L., 1972. *The Reference Other Orientation*. Carbondale: Southern Illinois University Press.

Schulz, Richard, 1978. *The Psychology of Death, Dying, and Bereavement*. Reading, MA: Addison-Wesley.

Schur, Edwin M., 1976. *The Awareness Trap: Self-Absorption Instead of Social Change*. New York: Quadrangle Books.

Schutz, Alfred, 1962. *The Problem of Social Reality*. The Hague: Nijhoff.

———, 1967. *The Phenomenology of the Social World*. Evanston, IL: Northwestern University Press.

———, 1970. *Reflections on the Problem of Relevance*. New Haven, CT: Yale University Press.

Schutz, Alfred, and Thomas Luckmann, 1973. *The Structures of the Life-World*. Evanston, IL: Northwestern University Press.

Scott, M. B., and S. M. Lyman, 1968. "Accounts." *American Sociological Review* 33 (February): 46–62.

Sennett, Richard, 1971. *The Uses of Disorder*. New York: Vintage Books.

Shaver, Kelly G., 1975. *An Introduction to Attribution Processes*. Cambridge, MA: Winthrop.

Sheehy, Gail, 1976. *Passages*. New York: Dutton.

Sheskin, Arlene, 1979. *Cryonics: A Sociology of Death and Bereavement*. New York: Irvington.

Shinn, Roger L. (ed.), 1964. *The Search for Identity: Essays on the American Character*. New York: Harper and Row.

Shott, S., 1979. "Emotion and social life: A symbolic interactionist analysis." *American Journal of Sociology* 84: 1317–34.

Simmel, Georg, 1950. *The Sociology of Georg Simmel*, ed. Kurt H. Wolff. New York: Free Press.

Simmons, R., J. Fulton, and R. Fulton, 1972. "The prospective organ transplant donor: Problems and prospects of medical innovation." *Omega* 3: 319–39.

Stein, Maurice R., Arthur J. Vidich, and David M. White (eds.), 1960. *Identity and Anxiety*. Glencoe, IL: Free Press.

Stoller, Robert J., 1968. *Sex and Gender:* Vol. I. New York: Aronson.

Stone, Gregory P., 1962. "Appearance and the self." In Arnold M. Rose (ed.), *Human Behavior and Social Processes*. Boston: Houghton Mifflin, pp. 86–118.

———, 1970. "Sex and age as universes of appearance." In Gregory P. Stone and Harvey A. Farberman (eds.), *Social Psychology through Symbolic Interaction*. Waltham, MA: Ginn-Blaisdell, pp. 227–37.

Stone, Gregory P., and Harvey A. Farberman (eds.), 1970. *Social Psychology Through Symbolic Interaction*. Waltham, MA: Ginn-Blaisdell.

Strauss, Anselm, 1959. *Mirrors and Masks: The Search for Identity.* Glencoe, IL: Free Press.
――――, 1981. Personal correspondence.
Stryker, Sheldon, 1968. "Identity salience and role performance: The relevance of symbolic interaction theory for family research." *Journal of Marriage and the Family* 30: 558–64.
――――, 1977. "Developments in 'two social psychologies': Toward an appreciation of mutual relevance." *Sociometry* 40: 145–60.
――――, 1980. *Symbolic Interactionism.* Menlo Park, CA: Benjamin/Cummings.
Stryker, S., and R. T. Serpe, 1982. "Commitment, identity salience, and role behavior: Theory and research examples." In W. Ickes and E. S. Knowles (eds.), *Personality, Roles, and Social Behavior.* New York: Springer, pp. 199–218.
Sudnow, David, 1967. *Passing On.* Englewood Cliffs, NJ: Prentice-Hall.
Szasz, Thomas S., 1967. *The Myth of Mental Illness.* New York: Delta.
Tajfel, Henri (ed.), 1982. *Social Identity and Intergroup Relations.* New York: Cambridge University Press.
Teitge, Dennis W., 1981. Viewing the construction of post-mortem identities. Unpublished paper.
Teitge, J. Smith, 1981. Self-realization and social estrangement: Employment and the gay dilemma. Unpublished dissertation: University of Notre Dame.
――――, 1982. Death work and the construction of post-mortem identity. Parts 1 and 2. *NRIC National Reporter* 5 (5 and 6).
Thoits, P. 1983. "Multiple identities and psychological well-being: A reformulation and test of the social isolation hypothesis." *American Sociological Review* 48: 174–87.
Tiryakian, Edward A., 1968. "The existential self and the person." In Chad Gordon and Kenneth J. Gergen (eds.), *The Self in Social Interaction.* New York: Wiley, pp. 75–86.
Turner, R. H., 1962. "Role-taking: Process versus conformity." In Arnold M. Rose (ed.), *Human Behavior and Social Processes.* Boston: Houghton Mifflin, pp. 20–40.
――――, 1976. "The real self: From institution to impulse." *American Journal of Sociology* 81 (March): 989–1016.
――――, 1978. "The role and the person." *American Journal of Sociology* 84: 1–23.
Walum, Laurel R., 1977. *The Dynamics of Sex and Gender: A Sociological Perspective.* Chicago: Rand McNally.
Warren, Carol A., 1974. *Identity and Community in the Gay World.* New York: Wiley.
Weigert, A. J., 1975. "Substantival self: A primitive term for a sociological psychology." *Philosophy of the Social Sciences* 5 (March): 43–62.
――――, 1975a. "Alfred Schutz on a theory of motivation." *Pacific Sociological Review* 18: 83–102.
――――, 1981. *Sociology of Everyday Life.* New York: Longman.
――――, 1983. *Social Psychology: A Sociological Approach Through Interpretive Understanding.* Notre Dame, IN: University of Notre Dame Press.
――――, 1983a. *Life and Society: A Meditation on the Social Thought of José Ortega y Gasset.* New York: Irvington.
Weigert, A. J., and R. Hastings, 1977. "Identity loss, family, and social change." *American Journal of Sociology* 82 (May): 1171–85.
Weinstein, Donald, and Rudolph M. Bell, 1982. *Saints and Society.* Chicago: University of Chicago Press.
Weinstein, E. A., and P. Deutschberger, 1970 (1963). "Some dimensions of altercasting." In Gregory P. Stone and Harvey A. Farberman (eds.), *Social Psychology Through Symbolic Interaction.* Waltham, MA: Ginn-Blaisdell, pp. 327–36.
Weisman, Avery, 1972. *On Dying and Denying.* New York: Behavioral Publishers.
Wexler, Phillip, 1983. *Critical Social Psychology.* London: Routledge and Kegan Paul.
Wheelis, Allen, 1958. *The Quest for Identity.* New York: Norton.

Wilshire, Bruce, 1982. *Role Playing and Identity*. Bloomington: Indiana University Press.

Zaner, Richard M., 1974. "Solitude and sociality: The critical foundations of the social sciences." In George Psathas (ed.), *Phenomenological Sociology*. New York: Wiley-Interscience, pp. 25–43.

Zijderveld, Anton C., 1971. *The Abstract Society*. Garden City, NY: Doubleday Anchor.

———, 1979. *On Clichés: The Supersedure of Meaning by Function in Modernity*. London: Routlege and Kegan Paul.

Znaniecki, Florian, 1965. *Social Relations and Social Roles*. San Francisco: Chandler.

Zurcher, Louis A., 1977. *The Mutable Self*. Beverly Hills, CA: Sage.

———, 1983. *Social Roles*. Beverly Hills, CA: Sage.

Index